Writing Well in the 21st Century

Writing Well in the 21st Century

The Five Essentials

Linda Spencer

ROWMAN & LITTLEFIELD
Lanham • Boulder • New York • Toronto • Plymouth, UK

Published by Rowman & Littlefield
4501 Forbes Boulevard, Suite 200, Lanham, Maryland 20706
www.rowman.com

10 Thornbury Road, Plymouth PL6 7PP, United Kingdom

British Library Cataloguing in Publication Information Available

Library of Congress Cataloging-in-Publication Data

Spencer, Linda, date
  Writing well in the 21st century : the five essentials / Linda Spencer.
    pages cm
  Includes bibliographical references and index.
  ISBN 978-1-4422-2757-6 (cloth : alk. paper) — ISBN 978-1-4422-2758-3
  (pbk. : alk. paper) — ISBN 978-1-4422-2759-0 (electronic)   1. Report writing.
  2. Language arts. I. Title.
  LB2369.S65 2014
  808'.042—dc23   2013045344

∞™ The paper used in this publication meets the minimum requirements of American
National Standard for Information Sciences—Permanence of Paper for Printed Library
Materials, ANSI/NISO Z39.48-1992.

Printed in the United States of America

To word people—that band of intrepid folks who study, write, and polish the written word.

CONTENTS

INTRODUCTION
Changes in American English

Developments in writing and printing technologies have had some influence on language usage in written documents since the invention of the first alphabet. The creation of an efficient system of printing using movable type, for example, influenced the development of punctuation in sentences. English, especially American English, and 21st-century technology are no exception to this interaction of language usage and technology.

Today, American English is a vital, growing, and changing language in the Digital Age. English ranks the number one language on the Internet, according to Internet World Stats. This worldwide user audience is changing English usage and style.

Keep in mind that American English is especially democratic. Everyday spoken and written usage determines what is correct and incorrect. There exists no American English academy like L'Académie française (the French Academy, founded in 1635). The Académie monitors and defines correct French, and it is the final word on French language usage. Common usage in speech and publications, both in print publications and on the Internet, determines acceptable American English usage. This book reflects that 21st-century usage. It is now acceptable, for example, to:

1. Begin a sentence with a conjunction: and, or, but
   Ida and Louis went to the marathon. *And* Casey stayed
   home.

2. End a sentence with a preposition
   When you left the library, what bookstore did you go *to*?

3. Use the plural pronoun referencing these words: everyone, everybody
   Everyone brought *their* lunches.

4. Close up prefixes, regardless of back-to-back vowels
   ant*ie*stablishment   ant*ie*litest

Yet despite all this change and growth of English, good writing still doesn't instantly happen, even on a computer screen. The most talented writer rarely has epiphanies when the words flow in perfect, poignant, and clear sequence. It doesn't matter if you are a student writing college papers, a working professional writing reports, a blogger, an essayist, or a novelist—everyone has to review, rewrite, and polish their writing.

Writers and Inventors

Writers are like inventors. Writers invent a document, story, article, or blog similar to the way inventors invent things. Inventors have an idea and then use materials such as metal, wood, or plastic to make that idea into a new item. Inventors then work on their inventions to improve their design and iron out the bugs to make the inventions work and be efficient and useful. This takes concentration and what Thomas Edison called "perspiration." Edison, who at the time of his death in 1931 held over a thousand patents for his inventions, knew what it takes to invent a useful item. He said, "Invention is two percent inspiration and ninety-eight percent perspiration." The idea is essential, but creating something tangible from an idea is equally essential.

Like inventors, writers invent or create something new: a story, a new idea, or an opinion—a cohesive narrative on a blank page using words. Writers also have to work to improve design and iron out the bugs to make their writing flow and be unique and interesting. This takes more than jotting down the first words that come to mind. Think of correcting and polishing writing as part of the essential, creative perspiration that Edison talked about. Developing an idea in words is just as creative as having the original idea. And often, when resolving writing problems and polishing writing, you have "aha" moments that inspire more ideas.

Perhaps when writing an essay, dissertation, college paper, or book, after you first get your ideas down and tackle the cleanup, you end up doing a third or fourth draft. At that point, often, the piece becomes "organic" to you. The spell-checker feature helps to reach a degree of writing correctness in spelling, punctuation, and to some degree grammar. But the spell-checker does not have critical thinking skills, and it does not understand syntax.

You know that each sentence can be written at least five different ways, but which of the five versions of a sentence is the best and should be kept? If you lack a specific approach to your creative perspiration, you can end up working on draft after draft and not complete any writing.

In this book, I urge writers when writing a draft and later doing the creative perspiration, the cleanup, to always examine their writing for the five essentials of good writing: punctuation, grammar, facts, mechanical and substantive style, and voice. I call this system PGFSV:

Punctuation
Grammar
Facts
Style
    Mechanics
    Substance
Voice

This system is basically the habit of thinking critically about the essentials of a written piece—punctuation, grammar, facts, mechanical and substantive style, and voice. In this book, I discuss each of these essentials in relation to 21st-century American English usage. This system helps you present your inspiration in its best written form.

Punctuation

Reviewing your writing for punctuation is a good place to begin. It might seem "small potatoes" when you think your job report, essay, blog, book, or thesis presents a revolutionary idea or new information, but the punctuation in your writing gives easy clues to sentences that need rewriting.

INTRODUCTION

Punctuation was not designed to confuse and frustrate writers. Punctuation was designed to create clarity and accessibility for the idea(s) expressed in a sentence. I will repeat this basic maxim throughout this book: If you know the basic punctuation rules and yet can't apply them to your sentences, then look to rewrite those sentences. Remember: Punctuation is supposed to *assist* in clarity—not obscure clarity.

Chapter 1, the punctuation chapter, reviews the basic usage of external and internal punctuation. The nuances of external punctuation—the period, question mark, and exclamation point—are discussed. The 11 internal punctuation marks—the comma, semicolon, colon, dash, hyphen, parentheses, apostrophe, quotation marks, brackets, ellipses, and slash—are also examined.

For internal punctuation, I give writers an option of using the system of close (*klōs*) punctuation or open punctuation. Most professional writers know they have this option in regard to their punctuation style. This option was routinely discussed in the style book used by the publishing industry, *The Chicago Manual of Style*. In the 15th edition of the book, however, the discussion of using an open or close punctuation style was unfortunately deleted.

This choice—which still exists in American English—is rarely taught in English classes. When writing a document—a job report, an essay, a blog, or a book—you need to choose which system of punctuation you are going to use. If you select close punctuation, then use as many internal punctuation marks as the rules allow. If you select open punctuation, then the opposite holds—you use as few internal punctuation marks as the rules allow.

Because commas seem to cause undue confusion for many writing in English, I've included a section in chapter 1 titled "Six Easy Commas." Examples are given for both the close punctuation system and the open punctuation system. Any consideration of such incorrect comma usage as a *breath comma*—simply inserting a comma when you pause reading a sentence—is ruled out.

Grammar

Grammar, like punctuation, does not have to torment you. If you have difficulty figuring out the grammar in a sentence, then the sentence probably doesn't work and needs correction. This is not to rain on your inspiration. But remember that once you've made an outline and then written the initial idea in paragraphs, writing is really a process of refining. When you think grammar, think parts of speech—nouns (proper and common), pronouns, verbs, adjectives, adverbs, conjunctions, prepositions, and interjections. Remember memorizing that list in elementary school?

Although all parts of speech are equally important, for clarity and flow I suggest you look first at the nouns/pronouns and verbs of each sentence. Are the nouns specific or general? Are the verbs in the passive or active voice? The active voice is preferred in the 21st century. Are you using too many adjectives and adverbs? Consider whether punctuation can replace a conjunction. And, lastly, do you use too many interjections to create enthusiasm in your writing?

Facts

With the advent of the Internet, no one needs to be sloppy in the facts they use. More information is available to you than you can possibly write about in your lifetime. Actually, the problem seems to be too much information. Primary and secondary sources are easily available with a click of the mouse. It is important that you use your critical thinking skills to determine the credibility of websites and the validity of the primary and secondary sources found on websites.

It is a global world; think about how you are presenting your facts. Are you citing facts with an American-centric or Eurocentric view? For example, suppose that I ask you: When did World War II start? If you answer December 7, 1941, your answer is wrong. I did not ask when World War II started for the United States. Your answer to my question must be inclusive. The fact is that World War II started in 1937 in Asia; in 1939 in Europe; and, for the United States, in 1941.

In chapter 3, I include tips on how to assess and determine the credibility of websites—an important skill in the Digital Age. No filters exist when doing Internet research. Filters? I do not mean filters to block unsavory websites. I mean that no filters exist to separate the websites that assess and vet the creditability of the facts that they present from those websites that do not. The Wikipedia website, for example, is not accepted by most publishers or academics as a creditable website, since the reference articles are not vetted. If I look to print books, I have the names of the books' publishers to guide me. I know, for example, that a reference book published by Random House would have more credibility than a reference book published by an unknown publisher.

A discussion of plagiarism, a common problem when using information from the Internet, includes examples that clarify what plagiarism is. A practice section at the end of chapter 3 helps readers identify plagiarized phrases and sentences in a document.

Style

Style has two parts: mechanics and substance. Mechanical style encompasses details such as how you style the numbers in your writing: Do you spell out all numbers, or do you follow *Chicago Manual of Style* and spell out numbers under 100 but use digits for those over 100? Or do you do what most people do in the 21st century and spell out numbers from one to nine and use digits for numbers thereafter? Whatever you choose, be consistent. Similarly, what specific words in the piece do you capitalize? Are you consistent? In this book, I capitalize *Internet*.

Substantive style is about the objective and tone of your writing. Ask yourself: What is the objective of the piece? What is the audience of the piece: print? the Internet? a specific age group? Does the piece you wrote have a slant or spin? What vocabulary will you use—formal or informal? Whatever you decide, be consistent.

Voice

Voice is the most elusive aspect of writing a piece. It is possible for a written piece to have a style, but not have a voice. But to have a voice in your writing, you must have a style. Do you put yourself into your writing? By *yourself*, I mean do you subtly express your values and views? Do you deliberately use certain vocabulary? And do you choose a punctuation style and specifically use the active voice? These are some of the questions considered in chapter 5, the voice chapter.

Style Sheet

You will be making many choices about punctuation, grammar, facts, and mechanical style in everything you write. Be consistent in your choices throughout each document. A Style Sheet is the best way to keep track of those choices. I recommend you make a Style Sheet for every paper, article, and document you write. Chapter 6 addresses what goes on a Style Sheet.

The Growing American English

Keep in mind that besides changes in usage, American English grows—new words are added every year to the Merriam-Webster Online dictionary. Because words are tools for writers, it is wise to keep abreast of new words added to English. A writer needs to select a dictionary to consistently use for reference. The dictionary that is provided in a word-processing program is not updated regularly and does not provide usage tips—dictionaries include more information than just spelling. The dictionary you select should be vetted, current, and one that regularly adds new words. I suggest you select a reputable online dictionary, as it would have the most current words and usage.

Words, Words, Words

American English especially absorbs words from other cultures at a rapid rate and has done so for centuries. For example, the Arabic words *abaya* and *burka* are part of American English and are frequently used today. But both words are cited in Merriam-Webster Online as being part of English since 1836, almost two centuries ago. It is just now in the 21st century that they are a part of common usage.

A new word more recently absorbed into American English is the Chinese word *qigong*. It is a noun indicating an ancient Chinese healing art that involves meditation, controlled breathing, and movement exercises. Merriam-Webster first included it in the dictionary in 2006.

American English also creates new words as people invent new objects and as new industries flourish, such as the high-tech software field rapidly expanding in the 21st century. The very familiar word *Google* is an example of this growth. The Merriam-Webster Online dictionary cites Google as a verb: "I will Google that." Usually capped, Google is also a name of a company and a computer search engine. The first known use of the word is cited as 2001.

New words recently coined include *robocall*. It is a telephone call from an automated source that delivers a prerecorded message to a large number of people. It recently was added to the Merriam-Webster Online dictionary in 2011. The word *copernicium*, a short-lived artificially produced radioactive element that has 112 protons, was first used in 2009 and made it into Merriam-Webster just two years after being invented. *Parkour* is another new noun. It means the sport of traversing environmental obstacles by running, climbing, or leaping rapidly and efficiently. It originated in French, which got a version of it from medieval Latin. It was first used in 2002, apparently in a James Bond movie. It also made it into Merriam-Webster in 2011.

A very useful new word for the early 21st century is the noun *mash-up*. It was first used in 1859, but in 2012 Merriam-Webster added a new meaning to the word. Today, it means something created by combining elements from two or more sources. A mash-up can be (a) a piece of music created by digitally overlaying an instrumental track with a vocal track from a different recording, (b) a movie or video having characters or situations from other sources, or (c) a web service or application that integrates data and functionalities from various online sources. A versatile word, it has lasted over a century, adapting to the times.

The Presentation of Information

Besides keeping abreast of new words and changes in usage, writers need to note that new technology changes how information is presented. Websites now present information in highly designed pages, often with boxed text, colored heads, short paragraphs, and bulleted lists. This change in the *form* of information also affects English usage.

Note that another form of communicating on screen in the 21st century is text messaging. A new form of English is emerging in this mode that is not explored here, but be aware that all new technologies in communicating affect how English, or any language, is used.

Clarity in the 21st Century

Despite new technology and the many changes in English language usage, clarity remains the goal of all writing. The frequent and age-old advice on how to achieve clarity is still true in the Digital Age:

- Each sentence needs a subject and a verb.

- Use active verbs, not passive ones.

- Use precise words—don't use sophisticated, unusual words just to impress the reader with your vocabulary.

- Limit the use of modifiers.

- Use credible facts from primary sources and vetted secondary sources.

Writing Well in the 21st Century: The Five Essentials gives you essential tools for writing with clarity in the 21st century. Use these tools and create well-written job reports, essays, course papers, dissertations, blogs, and all nature of books.

CHAPTER ONE

PUNCTUATION—THE CHOICES

Punctuation enables writers to convey clarity, nuances, feelings, pauses, and voice in their sentences. Punctuation was not designed to annoy writers or readers, although many people are, unfortunately, confused about how to correctly use punctuation.

Like most people, my introduction to punctuation was in elementary school. I particularly remember learning that punctuation was a series of rules. We practiced these rules on various sentences. The sentences had no connection to each other; we never practiced punctuating a paragraph or short essay.

I remember one punctuation rule: Always put a comma before a conjunction (*and*, *or*, or *but*) joining two independent clauses. We practiced this rule on various sentences with no emphasis on *why* we put a comma before the conjunction. We learned nothing about punctuation options.

We never discussed the role punctuation plays in a sentence—that punctuation is the writer's helper in creating clarity in a sentence, but also that punctuation helps convey the intangibles in a sentence: nuance, feelings, tone, and voice. Perhaps your experiences in first learning about punctuation were similar to mine.

In this chapter, I discuss the basics of punctuation and give sentence examples. I also discuss the essentials about each punctuation mark and what each mark conveys when it is used in a sentence. The options that writers have in how they use each punctuation mark is included. The practice section at the end of this chapter is a short essay, not a series of unrelated sentences.

A Punctuation Concept

Think of punctuation as a sentence necessity—every sentence has some kind of punctuation. The sentence "It's okay." has an apostrophe and end punctuation. The simple command sentence "Run!" has end punctuation. To become punctuation savvy, start noticing how punctuation marks are used in all the text you read. Once you start noticing punctuation in sentences, you will see that a sentence can have a variety of punctuation marks in it.

Consider the punctuation in the second sentence of this world-famous document, the Declaration of Independence.

> We hold these Truths to be self-evident, that all Men are created equal, that they are endowed by their Creator with certain unalienable Rights, that among these are Life, Liberty, and the Pursuit of Happiness—That to secure these Rights, Governments are instituted among Men, deriving their just Powers from the Consent of the Governed, that whenever any Form of Government becomes destructive of these Ends, it is the Right of the People to alter or to abolish it, and to institute new Government, laying its Foundation on such Principles, and organizing its Powers in such Form, as to them shall seem most Likely to effect their Safety and Happiness.[1]

Are the commas used here joining a series of phrases? Could a period replace the dash? Does the punctuation follow any rule you know? By the time you finish this chapter, you will be able to easily answer those questions.

Punctuation is a useful tool that can enhance your writing, and there are choices in how much punctuation you use. The more punctuation in a sentence, the slower people will read the sentence. The less punctuation in a sentence, the faster people will read the sentence.

Punctuation usage is still evolving, particularly in usage on the Internet. American English is a vibrant language, and just as English regularly acquires new words, so punctuation usage changes over time, especially with the development of new writing technology. In the 21st century, for example, the use of the dash in writing posted on the Internet seems to have increased; the use of the semicolon has decreased. It is now acceptable to write: "In the 21st century, the use of the dash has increased—the use of the semicolon decreased." Both the dash and the semicolon appear in this book.

You *can* master punctuation. There is a logic to punctuation. And if you are having trouble punctuating a sentence after applying the basic punctuation principles, ask yourself if the sentence is awkwardly written. I venture to say that 70 percent of the time when you ask yourself that question, the answer will be "yes." If the internal punctuation doesn't work, look to rewrite that sentence.

Essentials

1. Punctuation's job is to make a sentence read smoothly, have clarity, and convey feelings, nuances, and voice, and it can, subtly, add rhythm to a sentence. The more punctuation in a sentence, the slower the reader reads that sentence.

2. Punctuation rules do not exist to confuse people. Basically, punctuation falls into two main categories: *end* or *external punctuation* marks that end a sentence, and *internal punctuation* marks that fall within a sentence.

3. There are three external punctuation marks and 11 internal punctuation marks.

End or External Punctuation

As Garp says in John Irving's classical novel, *The World According to Garp*, "We are all terminal cases." Well, that adage also applies to sentences. All sentences and even fragments terminate. In English, you end a sentence using one of three punctuation marks:

period   .
question mark   ?
exclamation point   !

Each of the three end punctuation marks conveys a specific feeling, a kind of nuance. A period ends a sentence rather quietly and makes a definitive statement. Asking a question and using a question mark often get the reader's full attention. An exclamation point is emphatic and conveys much more emotion than a period.

The Period .

Essentials

1. Use periods to convey the completion of a thought. Thoughts are usually expressed in a sentence—a group of words that contain a subject and a verb.

> Ling ran for president of the senior class.
> Jennifer accepted the teaching job offered to her by Clemson University.
> Juan and Elizabeth joined the community gym and started a weekly exercise program.

2. Increasingly on the Internet, a period is used to mark the end of a fragment or entries in a bulleted list.

> Many students from American universities attended the international competition:
> • Lee Schooner, Abbey Chi, and George Pelosi from MIT.
> • Ahmed Levant, Beverly Stouffer, and Calvin Jones from Cal-Tech.
> • Michael Jacobs, Jen Kingsley, and Wayne Pierce from the University of Illinois.

The Question Mark ?

Essentials

1. The question mark always indicates a direct question. Sentences that are direct questions usually include one of the following words: did, when, what, where, how, why.

> Did Lin win the class presidency?
> When did Juan and Elizabeth join the gym?
> Why did Jennifer accept the teaching position at Clemson University?

2. Question marks sometimes are useful as *internal punctuation* for emphasis:

> Did Juan and Elizabeth work out on the treadmill? the rowing machine? lift weights?
> Did Lin get elected class president on the strength of her experience? popularity? aggressive campaign?
> Did Jennifer accept the teaching position at Clemson University for the salary? location? academic prestige?

3. Rhetorical or indirect questions do not end with a question mark.

> Her classmates wondered why Jennifer accepted the position at Clemson University.
>> Note the period here, although the heart of the sentence can stand alone as a direct question: Why did Jennifer accept the position at Clemson University?
>
> Students questioned what role Lin's popularity played in her election.
>> Note the period here. Again, the heart of the sentence can stand alone as a direct question: What role did Lin's popularity play in her election? How did Lin's popularity win her the election?

The Exclamation Point   !

Essentials

1. Use exclamation points in sentences and dialogue to express emotion and feelings—joy and happiness, excitement, astonishment, positive surprise, and even, in some cases, humorous irony.

> The Red Sox finally won the World Series!
> Lin was elected class president by one vote!

In dialogue:

> "I am thrilled to get into Oberlin's freshmen class!" exclaimed Sam.
> "Play ball!" shouted the empire.

2. Exclamation points do not express sadness or tragedy.

3. Exclamation points call attention to and emphasize a statement. Be careful, though—too many exclamation points can weaken your writing.

Fragments

Essentials

1. A fragment is one word or a group of words that does not contain a subject and a verb.

2. Usage of fragments, especially in Internet and electronic communication, is growing.

3. In the 21st century, it is okay to use one of the three forms of end punctuation at the end of fragments that actually do the work of complete sentences, even though the necessary subject and verb are absent.

Below are some fragments with different terminators and an explanation of what that end punctuation conveys. As you can see, each punctuation mark conveys how subtly a writer might want to communicate to the reader.

No.	Using a period here creates a rather quiet, reasoned reply.
No!	Using an exclamation point here creates more of an emotional reply.
No?	Using a question mark here communicates a doubtful reply.
What?	Using a question mark here conveys a clear question.
What.	Using a period here conveys a resolute statement.
What!	Using an exclamation mark conveys an emphatic, impatient reply.

Signage and the TV News Tickertape

We live in a world of advertising and signage. Those signs on billboards, electronic media boards, and advertising cards posted on buses and subways reflect, to a small degree, our culture's use of punctuation. Keep in mind that, whether on billboards, subways, buses, or electronic media, words and punctuation marks in advertisements are usually thought of as design elements. Periods, for example, are used indiscriminately. Look carefully at printed advertisements, and you will see there is little rhyme or reason to the capitalization and punctuation used.

Internal Punctuation

Internal punctuation is more complex than external punctuation. If you use much internal punctuation in a sentence, it slows down the reading of the sentence. Sometimes you want the reader to slowly read a document you have written, particularly if you are explaining a complex subject. Internal punctuation helps to clarify complex phrases in sentences.

Internal punctuation consists of 11 marks: the comma, semicolon, dash (1/n and 1/m), colon, hyphen, parentheses, ellipses, apostrophes, quotation marks, slashes, and brackets. These days confusion about punctuation, particularly commas, arises because no one discusses the two systems of punctuation and the differences between these two systems. *Chicago Manual of Style* used to discuss these two punctuation systems until its 15th edition, when for some reason that section was eliminated.

The two systems of punctuation are open punctuation and close (*klōs*) punctuation.

Open punctuation is using as few internal punctuation marks as possible in sentences. The internal punctuation used is absolutely necessary.

Close punctuation is using every internal punctuation mark that can be justified by a punctuation principle.

You have a choice or option whether to use open punctuation or close punctuation in your writing. Your making that choice is part of forming a writing style. The Punctuation Police do not decide for you. But the Punctuation Police do require you to be consistent in your usage in a written piece. Don't use open punctuation in the first paragraph and close punctuation in the second paragraph. Open punctuation is used more today, especially on the web, than close punctuation. If you are a student writing papers for your classes, however, usually you have to follow the punctuation style each professor determines. If you are writing reports for your employer, check to see if there is a company style. Often companies and organizations have a Style Sheet outlining the style of punctuation and grammar to use in all their written communications. See more about Style Sheets in chapter 6.

Commas　　，

The comma is the most frequently used internal punctuation mark. Commas slow the reader down—the more commas you have in your sentences, the slower the reader will read those sentences.

Essentials

1. The job of the comma is to help clarify the ideas in sentences and make the ideas accessible to the reader. Commas also add nuance, feelings, and voice to sentences.

2. There is no such thing as a "breath comma." Just because you breathe while reading a sentence doesn't mean you insert a comma.

3. As a writer, you have a choice between the two systems of punctuation—open or close punctuation—in your comma usage. As mentioned above, however, if you are a student writing class papers or an employee writing company reports, check to see if there is a school, class, or company style about comma usage.

Six Easy Commas

There are basically six different commas you need to know about. Below are the Six Easy Comma principles for close and open punctuation with examples for both systems of punctuation. Some of the commas are choice commas—depending on which system of punctuation you are using, you have a choice of whether to use that comma.

Beware: The One All-Important Rule You Need to Know

Never use a comma between the subject and verb in a sentence. The Punctuation Police will ticket you for this. The more tickets you have, the greater your failing grades or the less chance you'll get that job promotion. The only exception to this rule is when dates and addresses are used in sentences. You can put commas around dates and addresses even though the commas separate the subject and verb.

1. Series Comma—A Choice Comma

The series comma, or serial comma, is used when a series of two or more items occur in a sentence. The serial comma goes before the conjunction—the words *and* or *or*—that are used in the series.

This comma is also called the Harvard comma or the Oxford comma. The story of how this comma became associated with universities varies. The usual explanation is that both the Harvard University Press and the Oxford University Press once used the serial comma in their house styles. Today the names can cause confusion, so I call this comma its original name—simply the series comma or serial comma.

The passage from the Declaration of Independence that is quoted in the beginning of this chapter uses the serial comma. The comma joins a series of phrases.

The series comma or serial comma is a *choice comma*—you have a choice as to whether you will use it in your writing. If you use the serial comma, you are using the system of close punctuation. If you do not use the serial comma, you are using the system of open punctuation.

Close punctuation: series comma

Madeline and Ali went to the supermarket and bought oranges, bananas, *and* blueberries.
In this sentence, the comma before *and* is the series comma.
This sentence uses the close punctuation style.
Ling didn't know whether to buy the green, blue, *or* yellow sweater.
In this sentence, the comma before *or* is the series comma.

Open punctuation: no series comma

Madeline and Ali went to the supermarket and bought oranges, bananas *and* blueberries.

19

> In this sentence, the lack of a comma before *and* means this sentence does not use the serial comma. This sentence uses the open punctuation style.

Ling didn't know whether to buy the green, blue *or* yellow sweater.

> The lack of a comma before *or* in the series makes this an open punctuation style.

Both examples are correct. The Punctuation Police will not come after you if you choose to use open punctuation and no series comma. The Punctuation Police will come after you if you are inconsistent—using series commas on page 1 of your document but no series commas on page 5. Whatever punctuation system you choose, use that system consistently throughout the document you are writing or editing. A good habit to acquire is to keep a Style Sheet for the document you are writing and note on it what system of punctuation you are using. See chapter 6 for more about Style Sheets.

2. Compound Sentence Comma—A Choice Comma

The compound sentence comma is used to separate two independent clauses joined by a coordinating conjunction: *and, but,* or *or.* Each independent clause always has a subject and verb.

The compound sentence comma is a *choice comma*—you have a choice whether to use it in your writing, depending on whether you choose the close punctuation system or open punctuation system.

Close punctuation: compound sentence comma

> Madeline and Ali went to the store, *and* they stopped at the post office.
>> Here the comma and the conjunction *and* join the two independent clauses that are two complete sentences.
> On Saturday afternoon, Mei went to the football game, *but* she studied after the game.
>> Here the comma and the conjunction *but* join the two independent clauses that are two complete sentences.

Open punctuation: no compound sentence comma

> Madeline and Ali went to the store *and* they stopped at the post office.
>> Here there is no comma before the conjunction *and*. The conjunction works alone joining the two independent clauses that are two complete sentences.
> Mei went to the football game *but* she studied after the game.
>> Here there is no comma before the conjunction *but*. The conjunction works alone joining the two independent sentences.

Both of the above examples are correct, depending on which system you choose for your document: close punctuation or open punctuation.

Beware: The Wrong Use of the Comma in a Compound Sentence

The comma splice: Let's look at another opening sentence to a book that will probably be familiar to many of you.

> It was the best of times, it was the worst of times, it was the age of wisdom, it was the age of foolishness, it was the epoch of belief, it was the epoch of incredulity, it was the season of Light, it was the season of Darkness, it was the spring of hope, it was the winter of despair, we had everything before us, we had nothing before us, we were all going direct to Heaven, we were all going direct the other way—in short, the period was so far like the present period, that some of its noisiest authorities insisted on its being received, for good or for evil, in the superlative degree of comparison only.[2]

This sentence is the opening of *A Tale of Two Cities* by Charles Dickens. Is Dickens using commas in a series of phrases, or is he joining independent clauses together with only commas? If he is doing the latter, is it correct? Should he be using semicolons or conjunctions? Have you seen this style of punctuation in contemporary writing?

What Dickens did in this famous opening sentence is wrong! You cannot join independent clauses or sentences together in a compound sentence by just using commas. Using just a comma to join independent sentences together is called a *comma splice*. Such usage is incorrect, although some well-known authors have adopted it as part of their style.

21

The 20th-century writer John Updike, for example, was known for using the comma splice in his books.

Charles Dickens wrote *A Tale of Two Cities* in 1859, by which time he was quite famous and apparently his use of the comma splice was accepted. However, in your writing, particularly for academic papers, *do not use the comma splice.*

Beware: Do Not Confuse a Complex Sentence for a Compound Sentence

Complex sentence or compound sentence? Be sure to correctly identify a compound sentence. Remember that a compound sentence consists of two or more independent clauses usually joined by a conjunction. Each independent clause has a subject and verb.

Compound sentence: Harry and Shirley hiked in the Rocky Mountains for five days, and later they drove to the Pacific Coast in Oregon.

The subject of the first independent clause is *Harry and Shirley*. The verb is *hiked*. The subject of the second independent clause is *they*. The verb is *drove*.
If you are using close punctuation, a comma goes before the conjunction *and* as shown above.

Do not confuse a *complex sentence* with a *compound sentence*. A complex sentence has only one independent clause that is joined by a conjunction to a dependent clause(s).

Complex sentence: Harry and Shirley hiked in the Rocky Mountains for five days and then drove to the Pacific Coast in Oregon.

The subject of the independent clause is *Harry and Shirley*. The verb is *hiked*.
There is no subject in the dependent clause: *then drove to the Pacific Coast in Oregon*. That clause is *dependent* on the independent clause for a subject—that subject is *Harry and Shirley*. The verb for the dependent clause is *drove*.

This is a complex sentence and it is wrong to put a comma before the conjunction *and*. A comma before the *and* will wrongly separate the subject, *Harry and Shirley*, from the verb, *drove*, in the dependent clause.

Remember:
Compound sentence: two independent clauses joined by a conjunction and/or a comma
Complex sentence: one independent clause joined by a conjunction to a dependent clause

3. Introductory Modifier Comma—A Choice Comma

The introductory modifier comma is often used to set off a short introductory modifier of one word or a phrase. The introductory modifier comma is a choice comma—you have a choice regarding whether to use it in your writing, depending on whether you choose the close punctuation system or the open punctuation system.

Close punctuation: short introductory modifier comma

In 2013, Madeline and Ali attended the World Series.
Here in this close punctuation style, there is a comma after the short introductory modifier: *In 2013*.
Before Ralph graduated, he received a job offer from Apple.
In this close punctuation style, there is a comma after the short introductory modifier: *Before Ralph graduated*.

Open punctuation: no introductory modifier comma

In 2013 Madeline and Ali attended the World Series.
Here in this open punctuation style there is no comma after the short introductory modifier: *In 2013*. It is unlikely this clause will be misread.
Before Ralph graduated he received a job offer from Apple.
In this open punctuation style there is no comma after the short introductory modifier: *Before Ralph graduated*.

Depending on what system of punctuation you chose for your document (either close punctuation or open punctuation), the sentences above are correct. It is important that you select a punctuation system and then consistently apply it throughout your document. If you use open punctuation for the serial comma, you must apply open punctuation principles for the compound sentence comma and the introductory modifier comma.

4. Appositive Comma—A Necessary Comma

An appositive is a word or phrase that renames the noun preceding it or gives specific information about that noun. The appositive comma is a *necessary comma*. You need the appositive comma when using either the close punctuation system or the open punctuation system. The appositive, whether one word or a phrase, is *always* set off by commas.

The key to using the appositive comma correctly is identifying an appositive. A test for identifying an appositive is to mentally insert an equal sign before the word or phrase in question. Does the word or phrase equal in name or description the noun preceding it? Is the word or phrase necessary to clarify the description of the noun preceding it?

Close and open punctuation: necessary appositive commas

Madeline and Ali, *both noted professors at MIT*, live in Cambridge.
The phrase in italics equals the preceding nouns. The phrase is an appositive to the nouns, Madeline and Ali. The appositive comma is a necessary comma.
The 16th president of the United States, *Abraham Lincoln*, initiated the Emancipation Proclamation.
The name *Abraham Lincoln* equals the phrase *sixteenth president of the United States*—they are one and the same—so commas around the name are necessary.

In the two sentences below, the phrases or names in italics do not equal the preceding nouns or pronouns. The phrases or names are *NOT* appositives, so the phrases or names are not set off by commas.

Ali's sister *Fatima* graduated with top honors from Boston University.
No comma is needed. Ali has more than one sister; therefore, *Fatima* is essential to the sentence. Since Fatima is one of three sisters, the noun *sister* must be clarified.

Beverly and her office *colleague* Lee finished the marketing report within a week.

No comma is needed. Beverly has more than one office colleague and here the noun *colleague* must be clarified.

5. Nonessential and Essential Clauses—Nonessential Clauses Always Need Commas

Nonessential and essential clauses are also called nonrestrictive and restrictive commas. It is easier, however, to think of their usage in terms of nonessential and essential clauses in sentences. Nonessential clauses take commas. These are not appositives, as they do not equal the noun preceding them; rather they add some *nonessential* information to the sentence and therefore take commas. Essential clauses are just that—they provide *essential* information to the sentence and do not take commas.

Both the close punctuation system and the open punctuation system require these commas for nonessential clauses. These are not choice commas.

Nonessential Clauses   The key in deciding whether to use commas is to first identify the clause in question and decide whether the clause is essential or nonessential. Read the sentence without that clause.

The English language *which easily absorbs words from other languages* is the dominant language on the web.
The English language is the dominant language on the web.

The clause in italics (*which easily absorbs words from other languages*) is nonessential to the meaning of the sentence. The nonessential clause is set off with commas.

The English language, *which easily absorbs words from other languages*, is the dominant language on the web.

Read the sentence below.

The office of the president *which was established in 1789* is the highest elected office in the United States.

25

Is the clause in italics essential or nonessential? To decide, read the sentence without the clause in italics:

> The office of the president is the highest elected office in the United States.

The sentence reads clearly without the clause *which was established in 1789*. That clause is nonessential, so the clause takes two commas.

> The office of the president, which was established in 1789, is the highest elected office in the United States.

Essential Clauses   Essential phrases or clauses in sentences are *never* set off by commas.

Read the sentence below.

> The use of Internet communications *that began in the United States* soon spread to other countries.

Next, read the sentence without the clause in italics.

> The use of Internet communications soon spread to other countries.

Does the fundamental meaning of this sentence change if this clause is deleted? Yes—the phrase *that began in the United States* is essential to the sentence. No commas are used.

Read the sentence below.

> The number of businesses *that rely on Internet communication* has tripled in the last decade.

Then read the sentence without the clause in italics.

> The number of businesses has tripled in the last decade.

Does the fundamental meaning of this sentence change if the clause in italics is deleted? Yes—the phrase *that rely on Internet communication* is essential to what the sentence is saying. No commas are used.

Beware: Look Out for *Which* and *That*

Whereas both nonessential and essential clauses may begin with *which*, only essential clauses begin with *that*.

6. Miscellaneous Commas—Necessary Commas

Below are four examples in which miscellaneous commas are used—to emphasize a contrast, in addresses, in dates, and in a direct address.

A comma is used to emphasize a *contrast*:

Her speech was factual, yet interesting.
José was tired, but could not sleep.

In the 21st century, a dash is often used in such sentences instead of a comma:

Her speech was factual—yet interesting.
José was tired—but could not sleep.

A comma is used in geographical expressions and parts of an *address*:

Cambridge, Massachusetts, is the home of many students.
Des Moines, Iowa, is the location of Liam's business.

A comma is used in *dates*:

June 6, 2014, is Commencement Day at the University of Georgia.

But if the date is written in international style, commas are not used:

The new stock market building in Mumbai opens on 6 June 2014.

A comma is used in a *direct address:*

> "Thank you, Dr. Contini."
> "Marie, I know the answer to the question."

Semicolon ;

Usage of the semicolon has declined in the 21st century. Some grammarians predict that within 20 years, the semicolon will be extinct. Unfortunately, the semicolon is not frequently used in writing on the Internet. But it is still a viable punctuation mark with many uses and one to learn about and correctly use.

Essentials

1. Use the semicolon to join two independent *related* clauses that are not joined by a coordinating conjunction.

> The rain fell in sheets; the parking lot quickly flooded.
> The governor won most of the votes in the state's cities; she was easily re-elected.

2. Use the semicolon to separate two independent clauses joined by a coordinating conjunction when the independent clauses contain commas.

> In September 1939, Germany attacked Poland; and Poland's allies, Great Britain and France, declared war against Germany.
> The United States stayed out of the European war in 1939 and 1940; but it entered the war in December 1941, after Japan attacked Pearl Harbor in Hawaii.

3. Use the semicolon to separate dependent clauses in a series if the clauses are long and one or more of the clauses has interior punctuation.

> The Paris Peace Treaty ending World War I broke up old European empires and established new nations; turned the control of Middle Eastern nations, mainly on the Arabian Peninsula, over

to France and Great Britain; and called for the formation of a League of Nations, a world peacekeeping organization.

The Constitutional Convention held in Philadelphia, Pennsylvania, in 1787 established a federal government with legislative, judicial, and executive branches; devised a system of checks and balances among each government branch; and created a system for electing a president.

Note the complexity of the sentences requiring a semicolon. Often you will not find sentences with semicolons in newspapers online. Since people read more quickly on the Internet, overall, the sentences are less complex. Instead, dashes, colons, and commas are frequently used on the Internet.

Dash: 1/n or "En" Dash –
and 1/m or "Em" Dash —

The dash is a popular punctuation mark in 21st-century writing. Read an article or newspaper on the Internet and count the number of dashes in the piece. The dash is often used in place of commas, semicolons, colons, and parentheses.

Essentials

1. Two types of dashes exist in digital type: the en dash, or 1/n; and the em dash, or 1/m.

2. The 1/m dash is commonly called *the dash*. The 1/n dash is usually identified simply as a *1/n* or *en*.

The 1/n Dash

The 1/n dash is shorter than the 1/m dash, but longer than a hyphen. There are no spaces around the 1/n dash when it is used in a sentence.

1. The main job of the 1/n dash is to separate numbers.

In 1830–1860, Clarence Pickering owned a general store on Brattle Street in Cambridge, Massachusetts.

The quote from President Lincoln's speech appears on pages 9–11.

Phyllis plans to attend graduate school in 2017–2020.

2. Also use the 1/n dash, instead of a hyphen, between a prefix and a proper noun.

Marie wrote her PhD thesis about India in the post–World War II era.

Elsie studied at the state university in the pre–Depression decade.

1/m Dash

The 1/m dash is much stronger than a comma to set off a change of thought or to introduce a dramatic phrase. If you carefully read text on the Internet, you will see that the writing is full of dashes. Read newspapers and blogs and see how many dashes are used compared to semicolons or colons. There are no spaces around a 1/m dash when it is used in sentences.

1. The 1/m or em dash is used in sentences to show or describe a change of thought or action.

Tonight I want to do my homework—not.

Liu and Jason finished their dissertations—yet not in time to receive their degrees in this June's commencement.

2. In the 21st century the 1/m dash is often used to join independent compound sentences.

Erin bought a speed bicycle—and she bought an outfit to wear while bicycle riding.

Jim washed his car on Saturday—it snowed on Sunday.

3. The 1/m dash is also used to join informative phrases that used to be put in parentheses.

In the early 1400s, the Chinese explorer Zheng He—at the time unknown to most people in the West—sailed with his armada from China to Arabia.

The West African medieval nations—such as Mali and Ghana—were greatly influenced by Muslim traders.

Colon   :

The colon is the great *announcer* in punctuation. It tells the reader to Pay Attention! Important information is going to follow! That information usually is in the form of a list, a series of items, or a specific or lengthy quotation. The colon is used frequently on the Internet.

Essentials

1. As an announcer, a colon is used to introduce or announce a series of items, whether in a horizontal or vertical list.

> The banker wanted three financial statements: a credit report, last year's tax return, and a 401k statement.
> The coach shouted two words: score baskets.

2. The colon is used on the web to introduce a vertical bulleted list.

> In awarding the prize, the committee took into account:
> * The originality of the historical account
> * The facts included in the account
> * The sources of the facts cited
>
> This website includes the following:
> * Catalog of computers on sale
> * Location of store outlets
> * Online order form

3. The colon is used to dramatically emphasize phrases or words:

> The motivational speaker emphasized two words: college diploma.
> The quarterback had one word for his teammates: Win!

Hyphen   -

The hyphen is a *connector*. It connects compound words. Use the hyphen when you need to connect two or more words to form a compound noun or adjective. Increasingly in the 21st century, fewer words are being hyphenated and instead are simply being closed up and made into one word.

Essentials

1. Use the hyphen when you need to connect two or more words to form a compound adjective.

> Abdullah and Marian had a high-powered lunch with the CEO.
> Jack joined the award-winning soccer team.

2. Be able to identify open compounds and do not hyphenate them. An open compound is two or more words that form a unit, though they are spelled as two words. Open compounds are found in the dictionary.

> For homework, Mr. Arthur assigned chapters in two different *high school* textbooks.
>> The words *high school* form an open compound noun. The two words form a unit and are not hyphenated when used as an adjective.
> Steven's *coffee mug* holder on his car's dashboard broke.
>> The words *coffee mug* are an open compound noun. The two words are not hyphenated when used as an adjective.

3. Hyphenated compounds are always hyphenated and are in the dictionary.

> Ancient Athens was a successful *city-state.*
> On any summer evening we can see hundreds of *fire-flies* in our yard.

4. Temporary compounds are usually hyphenated and are used for a specific purpose. Temporary compounds are not often found in the dictionary.

> Deborah's *decision-making* skills gave her much success in the computer software business.
> The city of Chicago voted for the *low-cost* housing bond.

5. Closed compounds do not take a hyphen. They are usually found in the dictionary.

Alicia lost two chemistry *notebooks* when her *backpack* was stolen. Hari took a trip by *railroad* across northern Canada.

6. In the 21st century, instead of hyphenating prefixes in a word, such as

    re-pay   pre-nuptial

prefixes are being closed up:

    repay   prenuptial

7. The closing up of prefixes raises the issue of back-to-back vowels. Traditionally, when back-to-back vowels occur with the addition of a prefix, a hyphen has been used:

    anti-establishment   pro-active
    pre-election   re-emphasize

But today many dictionaries now favor eliminating the hyphen in back-to-back vowels.

    antiestablishment   proactive
    preelection   reemphasize

For clarity and to avoid reader confusion, I recommend the hyphen be used in prefixes when back-to-back vowels occur. It makes reading such words easier. This goes against Merriam-Webster Online, but the jury is still out on this question. In my reading, I estimate I find prefixes closed up just 50 percent of the time. Because this issue is still undecided, be sure you note on your Style Sheet how you handle prefixes.

Parentheses   ( )

When you interrupt a sentence with a phrase or complete sentence that *adds* to the subject of the sentence, use parentheses. In the 21st century, though, dashes seem to be doing the job of parentheses.

Essentials

1. Use parentheses around words, phrases, and even complete sentences that do not change the meaning of the sentence but add more information. Parentheses are always used in pairs. They are stronger than commas used around nonessential clauses.

Juan worked as an architect in Cairo (though he was born in Argentina) and designed many buildings in Cairo as well as Khartoum and Alexandria.

Allison was a successful businesswoman who owned a chain of designer shoe stores (inherited from her parents) that sold shoes throughout the world.

2. Use parentheses sparingly, as they greatly slow down the reading of a sentence. Because parentheses slow the reading of text, they usually are not used in web writing. Remember, we read text online differently than we read text on paper.

3. If you put complete sentences or phases at the end of sentences in parentheses, note the period placement in the examples below.

Hadi studied engineering at MIT and received a PhD from the University of Chicago and worked for NASA. (His PhD thesis was on building outer space telescopes.)

The U.S. college student population is predicted to grow in the next 10 years (by some 20 percent).

Quotation Marks   " "

When using quotation marks, be careful not to confuse the American style of using quotations marks with the British style. Below are examples of the American style.

In the 21st century in America, the usage of quotation marks has not changed. What has changed is how often people fail to use quotation marks when quoting someone's words. When researching a subject, keep careful records in your notes of those passages you quote verbatim. When you write your paper, be sure to use quotation marks appropriately and give credit to the person you are quoting.

Essentials

1. Use double quotation marks to indicate direct, precise words someone has written or spoken.

2. Always use quotation marks in pairs.

> "Let's take Route 95," she said. "It's quicker than Route 1."
> Jefferson wrote the words "When in the course of human events
> . . ." as the beginning of the Declaration of Independence.

3. In American-style punctuation, use single quotation marks for quotes within a quotation.

> "Jason simply replied 'no' when asked if he had a driver's license,"
> wrote Ralph Easton in the *Daily Sun*.
> "Judy Garland sang 'Over the Rainbow' beautifully," wrote movie
> star Shirley Tenney in her recent autobiography.

4. In American usage, periods and commas precede closing quotation marks—both single and double quotation marks.

> "George, it is obvious," said Alicia. "You have not read Robert
> Frost's 'The Housekeeper.'"
> "Ted," said the law professor, "please recite the first amendment
> that begins with the phrase 'Congress shall make no law.'"

5. In American usage, semicolons and colons follow closing quotation marks:

> I was assigned to write an essay about the lyrics to Paul McCart-
> ney's song "Eleanor Rigby"; instead, I wrote about the lyrics to
> John Lennon's "Imagine."
> Let's discuss the two opening lines of Emily Dickenson's poem
> "A Day": "I'll tell you how the sun rose, A ribbon at a time."

Ellipses . . .

The usage of the ellipses has not changed significantly in the 21st century. Be aware, however, that a digital issue about how to create ellipses does exist. Word-processing programs have a single ellipses character that consists of three dots. This single ellipses character is found under symbols. It looks like this: "Fourscore and seven ... this nation." But the recent *Chicago Manual of Style* calls for using nonbreaking, spaced periods that look like this: "Fourscore and seven . . . this nation." Most book publishers require the former in their printed and electronic books. Regardless of how you make ellipses digitally, the three dots must appear on the same line.

Essentials

1. Ellipses are a series of three periods used to indicate words, phrases, or sentences left out of a quotation. There are always spaces before and after ellipses. In the usage below, two sets of ellipses are used to indicate words or phrases that are left out of this quote. At the end of the quote, a period is used with the ellipses to show that this quote from the Declaration of Independence is incomplete and more text follows. Note the placement of that period.

> We hold these truths to be self-evident, that all . . . are created equal. . . . That to secure these rights, Governments are instituted among Men, deriving their just powers from the consent of the governed. . . .

2. In dialogue, you can use ellipses to show a pause or stoppage or an incomplete statement.

> "I am very happy to receive . . ." Shirley could not finish her acceptance speech.
> The father of the bride began his toast to the couple, "To my only daughter and new son-in-law . . ." but, overwhelmed, he could not continue.

Brackets   [ ]

Brackets are used mainly in quotations. Always use brackets in pairs and use them sparingly in quotations. If you are using a quotation that needs many brackets for clarity, rethink whether the quotation is being used appropriately.

Essentials

1. Brackets show that you have altered a quotation in order to explain, correct, or clarify the words in the quote you are using.

"[Amendment 1 to the U.S. Constitution] Congress shall make no law respecting an establishment of religion or prohibiting the free exercise thereof; or abridging the freedom of speech."

2. Use brackets for words you add or substitute in a quotation for clarification.

In describing John Adams, Thomas Jefferson wrote to his friend James Madison that "[He] is so amiable . . ."

3. Brackets are used to indicate when an error appeared in the original quotation, usually using the word [*sic*]. *Sic* is Latin that means "in this matter." When using the word in a quotation, put brackets around it and do not italicize it.

The Center for Disease Control announced, "As of Friday, 40 cases of bird flu were active [*sic*] in the United States."
Dr. Franck wrote, "At the Markus Diabetes clinic, after a year's treatment, 35 people were considered freed [*sic*] of diabetes."

Slashes   /

Use a slash sparingly. If your sentences require using many slashes, look to rewrite. If too many slashes are used in a paragraph, it makes the paragraph seem vague.

Essentials

1. Use a slash to indicate a choice or alternative. Do not put a space before or after the slash.

Each student voted his/her preferences for the most valuable student award.
The representatives decided to purchase the 60 vehicles from Acme Motors and/or Brookline Motors, if Acme Motors cannot deliver the vehicles on schedule.

2. A slash is now also used to show a range of numbers.

From 1990/92 the global stock market was volatile.
The bank's offices are open 9/5.

3. Slashes are used when writing fractions not found on the keyboard.

> Only 3/5 of the class members voted in the recent election.
> In his survey, Omar found that 3/4 of the registered patients at the clinic had health insurance.

4. Slashes are used in most website addresses.

> The URL for a good research website is http://www.bartleby.com/ Susan frequently visits the Project Gutenberg website at http://www.gutenberg.org/wiki/Main_ to read books from other nations.

Apostrophe   '

Apostrophes are still used in forming contractions, although there is some debate whether contractions should be used in writing for all audiences. Many think contractions give an informal tone to writing and should not be used in legal and scholarly writing. Contractions are rarely used in elementary school texts—both textbooks and readers. If you are writing reports for work or papers for school, check to see if your organization or school has a policy about not using contractions in written materials.

Essentials

1. Use an apostrophe to form a contraction—a shortened form of a word that substitutes an apostrophe for a letter.

> Jim can't go to the basketball game because he has to work.
> I haven't seen the latest political polls regarding her candidacy.

2. Use an apostrophe to form a possessive. The grammar chapter (chapter 2) discusses when to use the possessive and the various forms of singular and plural possessives.

> The Johnson's family dog won first prize in the dog show.
> Kenyatta's essay was published in a UN journal.

One Last Word about Punctuation

Remember that punctuation was designed to aid in writing sentences. Given that in American English there are three external punctuation marks and 11 internal punctuation marks, writers can write and punctuate any one sentence at least five different ways, each time creating a different feel and nuance. Consider:

Jolene Samuelson—a history professor at Oberlin—wrote a long, engaging, and popular historical novel about the many women who worked as spies in the Civil War.

Jolene Samuelson (a history professor at Oberlin) wrote a long, engaging and popular historical novel that was about the many women who worked as spies in the Civil War.

Jolene Samuelson, a history professor at Oberlin, wrote a long, engaging, and best-selling historical novel; it was about the many women who worked as spies in the Civil War.

A history professor at Oberlin, Jolene Samuelson wrote a long and engaging and best-selling historical novel about the many women who worked as spies in the Civil War.

A history professor at Oberlin, Jolene Samuelson wrote a long and engaging historical novel (which became a best seller) about the many women who worked as spies in the Civil War.

The next time you are writing or reading online, stop and think of the various ways the sentences you are writing and reading could be written and punctuated. American English gives writers many choices.

When reviewing punctuation in your document, ask yourself:

1. Does each sentence have a correct ending punctuation mark?

2. Did you use too many exclamation points to end sentences?

3. Did you consciously choose whether to use open or close punctuation?

4. Did you mistakenly use the "breath comma"?

5. Does the overuse of dashes make your writing choppy?

6. Is the same punctuation style consistently used throughout the document?

7. Does the internal punctuation enhance clarity in your writing?

8. Are all the internal punctuation marks in your sentences used correctly, including the correct spacing around these marks?

9. Read aloud your document. Does the punctuation work?

10. Did you record your punctuation style on the Style Sheet for your document?

Practice

Can you identify incorrect external and internal punctuation? Practice identifying punctuation mistakes in the brief essay below. Applying the close punctuation style for each line, briefly explain the incorrect punctuation mark. For lines in which the punctuation is correct, write "correct."

The Un-Broken Ring Circle

A. Before, the belief that garlic scared off vampires, the unbroken circle of a ring, according

B. to superstition, protected us from evil spirits. What evil spirits? Disharmony and

C. unhappiness. Naturally, that belief applied especially to wedding rings.

D. Wedding rings are worn in most cultures on the third-finger left-hand because

E. that's the "heart finger". It started with the ancient Egyptians. Supposedly a vein ran from

F. the heart to the top of the third finger on the left hand. Anything evil that touched that

G. finger would be felt by the heart. Whether that meant the touch produced heart

H.   palpitations, a heart murmur or heartburn is anybody's guess. But the belief was so
I.   strong that Greek and Roman physicians stirred medicines with the heart finger. If the
J.   portions were poisonous their hearts would tell them. That's rather iffy? Let's hope
K.   they washed their hands.
L.   Engagement rings are also worn on the "heart finger" . In European cultures,
M.   during the courting time followed after the giving of an engagement ring, the betrothed
N.   wore, the engagement ring on the third-finger right hand. During the wedding ceremony
O.   each bride moved the ring to her heart finger.

Notes

1. The Declaration of Independence, U.S. National Archives & Record Administration, accessed August 9, 2013, http://www.archives.gov/exhibits/charters/declaration_transcript.html.

2. Charles Dickens, *A Tale of Two Cities*, Literature Project, accessed August 9, 2013, http://www.literatureproject.com/tale-two-cities/tale2cities_1.htm.

GRAMMAR—CLARITY, CLARITY, CLARITY

Grammar is a system of how words are used in sentences and how words in sentences relate to each other. In order for sentences to express ideas or tell a story, words have to work together in sentences in some systematic manner. Learning grammar is learning that system. But parts of the English grammar system are complicated. You might have to read this chapter more than once! Remember, though, grammar is not designed to confuse people.

Grammar is much less stringent and more streamlined in the 21st century than it was, for example, during the Victorian era in the 19th century and even in the 20th century. Because of the development of computer technology, English grammar is changing in the 21st century.

We read and write differently on a computer screen than we do on paper. If you compare text from print books written before the Digital Age to text on web pages, you will find that, generally, most of the sentences in a web document are less complex compared with predigital print books. Shorter sentences seem to make up much of the content on websites. Also, the rules have been relaxed in the Digital Age. Despite what grammar purists say, in the 21st century it is now acceptable to start a sentence with a conjunction and to end a sentence with a preposition.

Whether your writing is for print or screen, however, you have to pay attention to grammar. Remember that writing is about building sentences with words. Each word in a sentence has a job. You can check what job a word has in a sentence by checking a dictionary.

For all your writing, you should decide which dictionary you are going to use from the many dictionary choices in the 21st century. People who write well don't rely only on word-processing dictionaries to check the spelling of a document. There are many more issues about words than their spellings. Select a well-known, edited dictionary. The American English lexicon has new words added to it yearly, and it is best to use a vetted and updated online dictionary.

Adopt the habit of checking your dictionary of choice to clarify more than the definition and the plural spellings of words. Dictionaries tell you what part or parts of speech a word is—some words in American English serve sentences in several different ways. The words *on* and *about*, for example, can be used in a sentence as adverbs, adjectives, or prepositions. The word *in* can be used as an adverb, adjective, noun, or preposition. Dictionaries online also include examples of sentences that show the correct usage of a word, and often dictionaries provide an update on any usage controversy regarding a word.

When reviewing the grammar of your sentences, remember that grammar is a system—a discernible system. If a sentence reads awkwardly, apply your basic grammar knowledge to the sentence and identify the job each word does in that sentence. If you have difficulty identifying the jobs the words do, look to rewrite the sentence. Remember that you can always write each sentence at least five different ways.

Grammar Concepts

Each word in a sentence has a job—one of eight jobs. Grammar is about using each word in a sentence in one of eight functions. To write well, you don't have to be a grammarian and know all the minute aspects of these functions. You do need to be able to identify what job each word in a sentence is doing and if the words are used correctly.

The eight types of jobs the words do in a sentence are collectively called the *parts of speech*. Some parts of speech are more important than others. Verbs are probably the most important part of speech. If there is no verb in a sentence, it is not a sentence. It is just a group of words, usually called a fragment. You will learn much more about verbs in the verb section.

In this chapter we will look at the eight parts of speech in sections. Words in sentences do basically four types of jobs:

Foundation words: Verbs, nouns, and pronouns
Describer words: Adjectives and adverbs
Connector words: Prepositions and conjunctions
The loner: Interjections

Some of these parts of speech are more important than others. As discussed previously, sentences must have verbs—this is a firm rule.

Each part of speech has various characteristics or traits. Don't get confused, for example, if a part of speech has several characteristics or classifications to it. We will start with the foundation words.

Foundation Words

Foundation words are the basic building blocks of a sentence—verbs, nouns, and pronouns. Without a verb, a group of words is not a sentence. I will say that again throughout this chapter. It is an important fact you should always keep in mind when you are writing anything.

Nouns name people, places, and things. That's important too. Think what the world would be like if we did not have specific words to name things. How, for example, would you talk about a computer if we did not have a name for the electronic wizard that now permeates all our lives?

Pronouns step in for nouns, which is very helpful in writing. Most grammar books begin with nouns, but I begin with the most important part of speech: the verb.

Verbs

Most grammarians consider the verb the most important part of speech. I agree with that, but I also think verbs are the most complicated part of speech. Don't let that deter you. Few people can name the future perfect tense (first person) of the verb *to be*. But it is important that you know the basics about verbs and how they work in sentences. When you are analyzing the grammar of your sentences, look first at the verbs. FYI: The future perfect tense (first person) of the verb to be is: *I shall have been.*

An important fact about verbs you should know is that a single verb alone makes a sentence. In these sentences below, the pronoun *you* is understood to be the subject.

Sing!
Dance?
Stretch.

Verbs have many different characteristics and traits. We will discuss the three major types of verbs and the five characteristics of verbs. Then we will discuss what some grammarians call the three "verbals"—verbs in sentences functioning as other parts of speech. But first we will look at the three major types of verbs.

Essentials

1. The three *types* of verbs are *transitive, intransitive,* and *linking verbs.* Most dictionaries will identify verbs as either transitive or intransitive.

2. Transitive verbs transfer or pass the action of the verb from the subject over to an object. Sometimes grammarians call transitive verbs *action verbs.*

> Maria *kicked* the ball. (subject: Maria; transitive verb: kicked; object that received the action: ball)
> Cato *organized* the report. (subject: Cato; transitive verb: organized; object that received the action: report)

3. The second type of verb is an intransitive verb. An intransitive verb does not transfer an action over to an object. There is no one or anything receiving the action. Intransitive verbs usually describe a condition or a state of being.

> Anne *sings* well.
> Jody *laughs* heartily.

Here is where a complexity arises: Sometimes the same verb can be used in a sentence as a transitive verb or used in a sentence as an intransitive verb.

> Anne *sings* that song well. (transitive verb, object: song)
> Jody *laughs* at jokes heartily. (transitive verb, object: jokes)

4. The third type of verb is the linking verb. A linking verb does not transfer action. It does not express an action. It is called a linking

verb because it *links* the subject, usually with a noun or an adjective. Because it does not transfer action, linking verbs are intransitive verbs.

The most common linking verb is the verb *to be* and its various conjugations: *be, being, been, am, is, are, was,* and *were*.

> The sunset *is* beautiful.
> They *were* happy!

The verbs connected to our five senses are often used as linking, intransitive verbs.

> The perfume *smelled* lovely.
> At midnight Virgil *heard* singing.

But they can also be used as transitive verbs:

> Maria *smelled* the perfume. (subject: Maria; verb: smelled; object: perfume)
> Ralph *heard* the bell. (subject: Ralph; verb: heard; object: bell)

Lists of other verbs that can be linking verbs can be found on the Internet. Some of those words are: *appear, grown, seen, turn, prove, remain,* and *stay*. Sometimes they are used in sentences as action, transitive verbs. See the examples below of the verb *to turn*.

> The audience's enthusiasm *turned* sour. (linking, intransitive—describes a state of being, a condition)
> The actor quickly *turned* the pages of the script. (transitive—the actor does the action, *turns*, and the pages receive the action)
> The actor *turned* suddenly. (intransitive—the actor does action, but no one or nothing receives the action)

Characteristics of Verbs

Verbs have five characteristics: number, tense, voice, mood, and person. These characteristics, or attributes, are often called the *properties* of verbs. Always look at the properties of the verbs in your sentences. All five characteristics are important, but pay special attention to the basics of number, tense, and voice.

CHAPTER TWO

Essentials

1. *Number*: Verbs are either singular or plural depending on the subject of the verb. Always make sure that the verbs in your sentences agree with the number of the subjects in the sentence. Ask yourself: How many are doing the action?

> *Wrong*: Juanita walk three miles a day.
> *Correct*: Juanita walks three miles a day.
>   The singular of the verb *walk* is *walks*.
> *Wrong*: The girls walks three miles a day.
> *Correct*: The girls walk three miles a day.
>   The plural of the verb *walk* is *walk*.

If the subject of the sentence is singular, the singular verb usually takes an *s*. If the subject of the sentence is plural, the plural verb usually does not take an *s*.

2. *Tense*: The tense of the verb identifies the time of the action of the verb. Basically, did the action or the condition take place in the past, the present, or the future?

> *Present tense*: Juanita *walks* three miles a day.
> *Past tense*: Juanita *walked* three miles yesterday.
> *Future tense*: Juanita *will walk* three miles tomorrow.

3. *Voice*: The voice of a verb is determined by whether the subject of the verb does the action or if the subject of the verb is acted upon. If the subject of the verb does the action, the verb is in the *active voice*. If the subject of the verb is acted upon, the verb is in the *passive voice*.

Overall, aim to use the active voice in your writing. Sentences written in the active voice tend to be clearer and more direct than sentences written in the passive voice.

A. Active Voice

In the active voice the subject of the sentence, whether singular or plural, or past or present, does the action of the verb.

> Sally *plays* on the softball team.
> Sally *played* on the softball team last year.
> Sally *will play* on the softball team next spring.

Sally, the subject of all three sentences, is doing the action—playing. Although in each sentence Sally is doing the action at a different time, all three sentences are in the active voice.

B. Passive Voice

In the passive voice, the subject *receives* the action. Another way to think about this is that the subject is acted upon. You create the passive voice using a form of the verb *to be—am, is, are, was, were, being,* or *been*—followed by the main verb's participle.

> *Participles*: All verbs have two participle forms: a present participle, which is the dictionary form of the verb plus *ing*, and a past participle verb formed by adding *d* or *ed* to the dictionary form of the verb.

Dictionary form of verb	Present participle	Past participle
flood	flooding	flooded
complete	completing	completed
use	using	used

> To make ice for the afternoon game, the hockey rink *was flooded* by noon.
> Fatima's latest book *was completed* in four months.
> The Internet *is used* for research by many scholars.

The passive voice is usually acceptable in scientific writing.

> Once the iodine *had been cooled* to 15° Celsius, the water *was added*.
> The facts of the scientific experiment are emphasized here rather than the person doing the experiment.

Most word-processing spell-checking programs can be set to search for passive voice verbs. The spell-checker will flag every instance of passive voice verbs—both appropriate (such as when the actor is unknown) and inappropriate. You need to decide whether flagged verbs should be active or passive.

Be sure to check your writing for excessive use of the passive voice. You will find that often when you are converting a sentence from passive to active voice, you might have to add a subject for the new sentence.

> *Passive*: The baseball *was hit* into left field.
> *Active*: Phil *hit* the baseball into left field.

4. *Mood*: The three moods of verbs are *indicative, imperative,* and *subjunctive*.

A. The indicative mood is the mood that states a fact or opinion or asks a question. Most sentences in American English are expressed in the indicative mood.

> The baseball team won five of its nine games. (fact)
> The pitcher needed a new glove to play effectively. (opinion)
> Will you encourage the coach to name a new pitcher? (question)

B. The imperative mood gives a direction, states a command, or requests something. Often the imperative mood sentence ends with an exclamation point. For more about exclamation points, see the punctuation chapter (chapter 1). The pronoun *you* is usually the implied subject of the imperative mood sentence. One exception to that is when the sentence is a direct address.

> Get the pitcher a new glove. (command; subject: you implied)
> Turn right at the next corner to reach the baseball park. (direction; subject: you implied)
> Please turn off the TV. (request; subject: you implied)
> Connie, be very careful when hiking the Appalachian Trail. (direct request; subject: Connie)

C. *Subjunctive mood*: The subjunctive mood expresses a possibility: something that is imagined, desirable or undesirable, or contrary to fact. Usually the subjunctive is found in a dependent clause introduced by words such as *if, though, lest, that, till,* or *unless.*

> The subjunctive mood is used when the verb expresses a possibility.
>> If you were to attend graduate school, you might get a job promotion.

The subjunctive mood expresses something imagined or contrary to fact.

> If I were wealthy, I could travel.
>> Using the subjunctive in this manner is stating that the "I" is not wealthy. The statement is contrary to fact.

And the subjunctive mood expresses a wish, a hope.

> I wish I were 10 years younger; then I could climb Mt. Helena.

People often ignore the rules regarding the subjunctive. When reviewing your writing always check whether any verbs are used, or not used, in the subjunctive. Note that when using the subjunctive construction, a comma follows a clause beginning with one of these words: *if, though, lest, that, until,* or *unless.*

Many American English grammarians claim the use of the subjunctive mood is declining. Perhaps it appears that way, or perhaps people don't understand its proper usage.

5. *Person*: This is the verb form that identifies whether the subject of the sentence is doing the speaking, is spoken to, or is spoken about. A common verb form, writers use it almost automatically.

> The subject doing the speaking:
>> *I will bake* three cakes for the party.
>> Following the playwright's instructions, *I skip* down the driveway.
> The subject spoken to:
>> *You bake* three cakes for the party.
>> Following the playwright's instructions, *you skip* down the driveway.
> The subject spoken about:
>> *They will bake* three cakes for the party.
>> Following the playwright's instructions, *they skip* across the stage.

6. *Gerunds, participles, and infinitives*: These forms of verbs can be complicated to identify in sentences. Grammarians call these forms of verbs *verbals*. A verbal is a word that is formed from a verb but works in a sentence as a different part of speech.

A. Gerunds are verbs with an *ing* ending, and they work as nouns in sentences. The action is ongoing.

> *Singing* is Celeste's life. (*Singing* is the subject.)
> Marian hates *cooking*. (*Cooking* is the direct object.)

B. Participles are verbs with an *ing* or *ed* ending, and they work in sentences as adjectives or adverbs. If the participle ends in *ing*, the action is ongoing.

> *Hearing* him perform Mozart, I feel happy again.

If the participle ends in *ed*, then the action has passed. Add *ed* to the base of the verb.

> He danced his way through many films, *revered* by every film critic.

C. Infinitives are verbals that can do the job of a noun (like a gerund) and can also do the job of an adjective or adverb (like a participle). Infinitives are easy to spot in sentences since they always use the word *to* before a verb.

> *To cook* is Jane's greatest pastime. (subject)
> Harriet ran every day *to lose* weight. (adverb)

Nouns

Nouns are one of the common building blocks of a sentence. There are five essentials you should know about nouns. These essentials range from the types of nouns in American English to the plural and possessive forms of nouns.

Essentials

1. Nouns name persons, places, things, feelings (often called *qualities*), and ideas in sentences.

> *Persons*: *Fredericka* won first prize in the swimming meet.
> *Places*: The political representatives met in *Des Moines, Iowa*.
> *Things*: Kimberly bought a new soccer *ball*.

Feelings: Smiles of *joy* covered the faces of attendants in the wedding procession.

Ideas: In the 21st century, *democracy* spread throughout the world.

2. Different types of nouns exist:

A. *Proper nouns*: names of persons, places, or things:

Fatima Hassan   Kansas   Statue of Liberty
   Proper nouns are capitalized.

B. *Common nouns*: general names of things, objects, feelings, and ideas:

flag   desk   joy   democracy

   Common nouns are often sorted into three types:

a. *Concrete nouns*: things that you see or perceive through the five senses:

computer (see)   perfume (smell)   humidity (feel)
symphony (hear)   garlic (taste)

b. *Abstract nouns*: things you cannot see—ideas, feelings, or conditions:

fear   happiness   excitement   intensity

c. *Collective nouns*: these identify a group of people or things:

team   audience   class   club
Collective nouns usually take the singular verb.

FYI: A nomenclature of collective nouns for animals developed in British English from the 1300s through the 1500s. These collective nouns were used especially in hunting societies in England, and knowledge of these words often indicated you were educated and a member of the upper class. You can find various lists of these words on the Internet. Writers in the 21st century often use these words for effect, such as a *gaggle of geese* instead of flock of geese, a *shoal of fish* instead of a school of fish, and a *clutch of hens* instead of a brood of hens.

3. Basically, in a sentence, a noun does the action described by a verb, or a noun describes a condition or a state of being. This makes a noun the subject of a sentence. Nouns and verbs, together, are the most common parts of speech in sentences.

Aysi ran in the marathon last year.

>*Aysi* is the noun doing the action and therefore the subject of the verb *ran*.

Liberty is the subject of the Declaration of Independence.

>The noun *liberty* describes a condition or a state of being and is the subject of the verb *is*.

4. Noun plurals have different forms.

A. Do *NOT* use an apostrophe and *s* (*'s*) to make a noun plural. Most nouns form plurals by adding just an *s* to the singular noun.

carnival, carnivals	table, tables
officer, officers	house, houses

B. Some nouns ending in *f* or *fe* form the plural by changing the ending to *ve* before adding an *s*:

leaf, leaves	wife, wives
life, lives	yourself, yourselves

C. Singular nouns ending in *s, sh, ch,* or *x* form the plural by adding *es*:

kiss, kisses	church, churches
wish, wishes	Jones, Joneses

This means that the plural of *Charles* is *Charleses*. Since this is so awkward, look to rewrite your sentence.

>*Awkward*: All the Charleses gathered on Saturday evening for a barbecue.
>
>*Better*: On Saturday evening all members of the Charles family gathered for a barbecue.

D. Nouns ending in *o* in which the *o* is preceded by a consonant usually form the plural by adding *es*.

hero, heroes   tomato, tomatoes

E. If a word ends in *y* and the *y* is preceded by a vowel, add *s*:
chimney, chimneys
journey, journeys

F. If a word ends in *y* and the *y* is preceded by a consonant, drop the *y* and add *ies*:

opportunity, opportunities
story, stories

G. To make the plural of numbers and letters, simply add *s*:
the 1960s   AAAs

In the past, some debate occurred about whether to use an apostrophe to make numbers and letters plural: 1960's or AAA's. The majority of usage in the 21st century removes the apostrophe and just adds the *s*, as the example above shows.

5. Noun possessives have different forms for the possessive noun singular and the possessive noun plural.

A. Singular noun possessives
To form the possessive noun singular, add *'s* to the singular noun form.
Juanita's dog won the first prize at the dog show.
The *lion's* tail was mangy.

To avoid creating awkward usages when using the singular possessive noun, always look to rewrite.
Awkward: People still read Keats's poems in the 21st century.
Better: In the 21st century, people still read poems by Keats.

B. Noun plural possessives
First, make the noun plural and then add only an apostrophe to plural nouns ending in *s* or *es*.

Singular	Plural	Plural possessive
planet	planets	planets'
car	cars	cars'
James	Jameses	Jameses'

The *planets'* locations in the universe are unknown.
The company recalled all the *cars'* engines.

Noun plural possessives can often make for awkward sentences when the singular form of a word ends in *es*, such as James listed above. And consider the difficulty of the plural possessive for Charles, which is *Charleses'*. You should definitely rewrite to avoid using the plural possessive of proper nouns that end in *es*.

Awkward: The *Jameses'* talents are extraordinary.
Better: The *James* family has extraordinary talent.

Add *'s* for the possessive to plural nouns not ending in *s*:

The law establishes *children's* rights.
Publicity about the incident grabbed the *women's* attention.

Recap: To make the singular possessive, add an *'s*. To make the plural possessive, make the plural of the noun, and if it ends in *s*, add just an *apostrophe*.

Singular possessive:
Awkward: In the 1600s, King Charles's reign in England was eventful.
Better: In the 1600s, *the reign of King Charles* in England was eventful.
Plural possessive:
Awkward: The two Charleses' reigns in England were eventful.
Better: The two English kings *named Charles* had eventful reigns.

Pronouns

Think of pronouns as stand-ins for nouns. The definition of pronouns in Merriam-Webster is "any of a small set of words in a language that are used as substitutes for nouns or noun phrases." The definition goes on to say that the *who* or *what* that each pronoun refers to is named or understood in the context. That is an important element in learning about pronouns. Pronouns refer to or replace nouns—but those nouns are either named or understood in the context of the sentence or paragraph. When you use a pronoun in a sentence, either it must have a reference or the pronoun's reference must be understood from the content in which it is being used.

Brian won first prize in the writing contest, and *he* used the prize money to travel to Europe.

Eliza reported on events in *Ghana* for the United Nations; *she* lived *there* for three years.

In the sentence above, *she* refers to Eliza and *there* refers to Ghana.

In the paragraph below, it is clear that the *he* and *his* pronouns refer to Derrick.

In the 2012 election year, Derrick had traveled to Iowa to cover presidential primary campaigns for NPR. There *he* worked long hours, attending one campaign speech to another. Though *he* worked hard in Iowa that year, *he* met the woman who would eventually become *his* wife.

Essentials

1. Different categories of pronouns exist. An ongoing debate among grammarians over the number of categories of pronouns continues in the 21st century, but in this chapter, six categories of pronouns are identified and discussed.

A. *Personal pronouns*: Personal pronouns come in three types or cases: nominative, objective, and possessive.

a. Nominative pronouns are always the subject of a verb.

I	we
you	you
he, she, it,	they

They went to the first baseball game played in the new stadium. *You* and *I* can communicate through email when you are traveling.

Nominative pronouns always follow the verb *to be*. In conversation, we usually use the objective case: It is *me*. But in formal writing, use the correct usage: It is *I*.

When using *as* or *than* in making a comparison, select the pronoun that would finish the clause:

Max wanted to stay out later than *she*. (than she did)

b. Objective pronouns are never the subject of a verb but always the object of a verb, preposition, or infinitive.

me	us
you	you
him, her, it	them

Michael gave *him* the class notes for the biology class. (object of the verb)

She drove with *her* to the amusement park. (object of the preposition)

Joyce wanted the chef to cook *her* a different meal. (object of the infinitive)

c. Possessive pronouns always show ownership and answer the question: Whose?

mine	ours
yours	yours
his, her, its	theirs

The new car in the driveway belongs to *her*. (Whose car? *her* car)

I think the results of the essay contest are fair since *mine* won first prize and *yours* won second prize. (Whose essays? *mine*, *yours*)

B. *Relative pronouns*: These pronouns join a dependent clause to the main, independent clause of the sentence. Relative pronouns always stand in for a specific noun in the sentence. They are *which*, *that*, *who* (or *whom* if the objective form should be used).

Marie is a woman *who* will succeed in the business world.

The pronoun *who* points back to Marie. The phrase *who will succeed in the business world* is the dependent subordinate clause.

Rules for relative pronouns:

a. Use the nominative case *who* when the pronoun is the subject of a verb.

Nathan wondered *who* was driving the red sports car.

The pronoun *who* is the subject of *was driving*.

Who do you think won the school prize?

The pronoun *who* is the subject of *won*.

b. Use the objective case *whomever* when the pronoun is the object of a verb, preposition, or infinitive.

Cherie went to the basketball game with *whomever* asked her first.

The pronoun *whomever* is the object of the preposition *with*.

Heidi decided to give the bag of groceries to *whomever* she saw at the shelter.

The pronoun *whomever* is the object of the preposition *to*.

c. Use *whom* and *who* only to refer to people. *That* is used to refer to animals and things.

Jonathan, *who* won the swimming meet, appeared in the sports DVD.

The pet tiger *that* escaped from the zoo roamed the neighborhood.

C. *Reflexive pronouns*: These pronouns reflect the action of the verb back to the subject. Some grammarians call reflexive pronouns *mirror pronouns* because they usually reflect back to a noun or pronoun. They are often used for emphasis.

myself	ourselves
yourself	yourselves
himself	themselves
herself	
itself	

The publicity teams worked *themselves* into exhaustion preparing for the political convention.

The president, *herself*, announced the military base was closing.

Ian gave *himself* a car.

D. *Demonstrative pronouns*: These pronouns point to the thing you are talking about in the sentence. Always make sure the pointing word is standing in for a noun. If not, then the word is an adjective.

this	these
that	those

Beware: Do not confuse and misuse *that* and *which*. See the punctuation chapter (chapter 1) under essential and nonessential clauses.

Jason bought Beverly *that* blue 10-room house on Elm Drive.

The trees, *which* Harry planted long ago, need to be trimmed.

E. *Interrogative pronouns*: Perhaps the easiest pronouns to identify, interrogative pronouns ask a question.

which
who/whom
what

What book did the professor want students to read over spring break?

Who finished the New York City marathon first?

Whom did Henry give the book to?

See the section on prepositions about ending sentences with a preposition.

F. *Indefinite pronouns*: Indefinite pronouns are general and vague pronouns. They do not stand for specific nouns in a sentence. Often they are the subject of a sentence. Various lists ranging from 10 to 40 indefinite pronouns appear in grammar books and on grammar websites. Below is a list of the more common indefinite pronouns. Familiarize yourself with these pronouns.

some	several	many
few	all	both
none	everyone	everybody
neither	nobody	

Beware: Some indefinite pronouns once took singular possessive pronouns. Example:

Everyone brought *his* lunch to the meeting.

This establishes *everyone* as male. In order to define everyone as gender neutral, in the 21st century it is permissible and usual to say:

Everyone brought *their* lunches to the meeting.

When confronted with this issue, it is a good time to remember that every sentence can be written at least five different ways. If the grammar presents a problem, in this case the pronouns, look to rewrite the sentence:

Everyone brought lunches to the meeting.
Everyone brought a lunch to the meeting.

FYI: While the use of the singular indefinite pronoun with a plural pronoun to avoid gender bias is now accepted use in the 21st century, Fowler's actually quotes this usage back to 1877.

Describer Words

There are two types of describer words in American English: adjectives and adverbs. Basically adjectives describe nouns and pronouns and adverbs describe verbs, adjectives, and other adverbs.

Grammarians often describe adjectives and adverbs as words that "qualify" other parts of speech. What they mean by "qualify" is that adjectives and adverbs describe, or make more specific, other parts of speech.

When you are looking at the grammar in your sentences, it is important you remember that adjectives always and only describe nouns and pronouns, and adverbs always and only describe verbs, adjectives, and other adverbs.

Adjectives

Adjectives are words that describe, or modify, nouns and pronouns. Adjectives tell more about the nouns and pronouns in a sentence and help make nouns or pronouns more specific. In sentences, adjectives usually are placed just before the nouns or pronouns they are describing.

In any discussion of adjectives, it is always pointed out that adjectives usually answer one of three questions about a noun or pronoun.

61

The *luxury* car sped down the highway. (*Which* car?)

The *state* legislature vetoed the bill that required *bicycle* lanes on highways. (*What type* of legislature and *what type* of lanes?)

Six undergraduates participated in the college triathlon. (*How many* undergraduates?)

Adjectives are a relatively easy part of speech to understand, as, for example, compared to verbs. Adjectives have only one characteristic—but it is a very helpful characteristic for writers.

Essentials

1. Adjectives describe only nouns and pronouns. If you are unsure whether a word is an adjective, look to see what word it is describing. If that word is a noun or pronoun, the word describing that noun or pronoun is an adjective.

> Bertha's painting won the *silver* prize for excellence in the art show.
>
> Aaron swam every day to prepare for the *three* swim meets.

2. Adjectives have one primary characteristic that is very useful in writing. That characteristic is comparison. Adjectives can convey the degree or gradations of a noun or pronoun. Sometimes adjectives change form in doing this, but other times they do not.

> There are two degrees: comparative and the superlative. The comparative is used when talking about two items or people. The superlative is used when talking about more than two items or people. Most one-syllable adjectives usually use the ending *er* when forming the comparative and *est* when forming the superlative.
>
> > Greta had *bluer* eyes than her brother. (comparative: *bluer*, comparing the eyes of two people)
> >
> > Molly had the *reddest* hair of the four girls in the family. (superlative: *reddest*, comparing the hair of more than two people)
>
> Adjectives with more than one syllable usually use *more/less* for the comparative and *most/least* for the superlative comparison.

Of the two paintings, Juan's *more beautiful* painting of a sunset won the prize.

Mildred's *least favorite* subject was college physics.

3. Some adjectives have irregular comparison.

Adjective	Comparative	Superlative
good	better	best
bad	worse	worst
much	more	most
many	more	most
little	less	least

Martin hit the *most* home runs of the season.

Wanda did *better* on the math exam than Calvin.

If you are unsure of how to form the comparison of a word, check the dictionary.

4. Some adjectives are absolutes; they cannot be compared. One of the most common absolute adjectives is *unique*:

Wrong: The painting of Cairo was the *most unique* painting in the exhibition.

Correct: The painting of Cairo was the *unique* painting in the exhibition.

The painting cannot be *more unique* or *less* unique. It is simply unique.

Wrong: Roy's final grade in biology was more *sufficient* for him to graduate.

Correct: Roy's final grade in biology was sufficient for him to graduate.

The grade cannot be more *sufficient*. It is simply *sufficient*.

Lists of other common adjectives that usually are treated as absolutes and do not take comparisons are on the Internet. Below are the ones frequently used.

chief	false	preferable
complete	ideal	void
dead	impossible	whole

5. Phrasal adjectives, often called compound adjectives, should be placed before the noun they are describing and be hyphenated.

> The petition for more money by the school superintendent was called an *over-the-top* request by the mayor.
>
> Sonia's electronics store is the *fastest-growing* business in the mall.

Adverbs

Adverbs also describe or modify parts of speech. They tell more about or make more specific words that are verbs, adjectives, or other adverbs. In your sentences, place adverbs as close as possible to the words they modify.

> She smiled *happily*. (describing a verb)
> Juan was *under* 21. (describing an adjective)
> I know that all *too* well. (describing an adverb)

Adverbs never describe or tell more about nouns or pronouns. If you are unsure a word is an adverb or an adjective, look at the word it is describing. You can also check a dictionary, which will tell you whether the word is an adverb or an adjective or other part of speech.

Essentials

1. *Questions that adverbs answer*: In their telling more about verbs, other adverbs, or adjectives, adverbs usually answer the questions: Where? When? How? And to what extent or degree?

> Sergeant Gates soon turned *right* onto Route 65. (*Where* did he turn?)
> Yesterday, Sandra ran the marathon. (*When* did she run?)
> Valerie quickly finished her chemistry course. (*How* did she finish?)
> Julia thought the drama was less than convincing. (To *what* degree?)

2. *ly endings*: Many adverbs end in *ly*, such as *mainly*, *quickly*, and *slowly*.

Theodore *quickly* ran to the drugstore. (*How?*)
Abigail *slowly* memorized the verb conjugation in the lesson.
(How?)

However, not all adverbs end in *ly*; common adverbs that do not end
in *ly* include the following: fast, very, well, quite, late.

Leah did *very* well on the final history exam. (To *what* degree?)
Juan arrived *late* to the exam. (*When?*)

Again, if you are unsure of whether a word is an adverb in your sentence, identify the word it describes. Is that word another adverb, a
verb, or an adjective? If you are still not sure, check that word in a
dictionary to see what part of speech it is.

3. *Adverbs and verbs*: One of the jobs of the adverb is to make verbs
more specific. It is your writer's choice to decide how specific you
want the verbs you use to be. Good writing uses specific verbs, and
some verbs seem to demand that you use an adverb to make the verb
more specific. Such verbs as *act*, *conduct*, and *operate* are neutral verbs
and need clarification to describe whether positive or negative action
was taken.

Vague: Katherine Bertolli *conducted* Beethoven's Ninth Symphony.
Specific: Katherine Bertolli *vigorously conducted* Beethoven's Ninth
Symphony.
Vague: Jason operated the truck through the blizzard.
Specific: Jason *deftly operated* the truck through the severe blizzard.

A. Compound verbs and adverbs: When an adverb is used to describe a compound verb, its proper place is between the auxiliary
and the rest of the verb.

José was *quickly* eating breakfast in the cafeteria when the fire
alarm sounded.
This semester, Cynthia has *suddenly* dropped out of Spanish class.

4. *Comparatives*: Most one-syllable adverbs show degrees of comparison by using the ending *er* and *est*, the same way that adjectives form
comparisons.

Adverb	Comparative	Superlative
slow	slower	slowest
fast	faster	fastest

Words of more than one syllable usually use *more/most* or *less/least*.

Adverb	Comparative	Superlative
lovely	more or less lovely	most or least lovely
quickly	more or less quickly	most or least quickly

Of all the women at the gathering, Bob thought Mona looked the *most lovely*.

You have to agree that the tortoise moved *less quickly* than the hare.

A. Irregular adverb comparatives: Some adverb comparatives use different words in the comparative and superlative degrees:

Adverb	Comparison	Superlative
well	better	best
badly	worse	worst

Check a dictionary for the adverb comparative of specific words.

Jason did the *worst* in the class singing competition.

Amy played the piano *better* than her sister at the recital.

5. *Adverbial phrases and adverbial clauses*: Adverbial phrases and clauses consist of more than one word and are used like individual adverbs—they describe or modify verbs, adjectives, and other adverbs. These phrases and clauses answer the same questions as individual adverbs: Where? When? How? And to what extent or degree?

It is very hot and humid in countries near the Equator. (*Where?*)

Every time he opened the skylight, a bat flew into the house. (*When?*)

Jason walked into the company headquarters *like he owned it*. (*How?*)

Cathy was not as honest *as we all thought*. (To *what* extent or degree?)

Connector Words

The connecting words do an important job—they join together the various nouns, pronouns, verbs, adverbs, and adjectives into a coherent whole and a sentence is formed. There are only two types of connector words.

Prepositions

Prepositions are connectors in sentences. They usually connect nouns and pronouns to other words in the sentence. Often the nouns and pronouns connected are the objects of the prepositions. They are also sometimes used to connect a verb, adjective, or adverb and even phrases and clauses.

> Manuel ran *in* the marathon. (connects noun)
> Lin gave the book *to* me. (connects pronoun)

Grammarians warn against overusing prepositions and suggest always checking your writing for too many prepositions. Be careful that any use of prepositional idioms is correct. Lists of prepositions and prepositional idioms are on the Internet.

Essentials

1. Prepositions never change form; there are no comparisons for prepositions.

2. It is okay to end a sentence with a preposition. I say this with some conviction, even though purists still debate this issue in the 21st century. Some insist that writers rewrite sentences to avoid a preposition at the end. But most of the time the rewrite of the sentence is so convoluted that it is better, for the sake of clarity, to end a sentence with a preposition.

> *Bad*: Ray did not know *to* where he was driving.
> *Better*: Ray did not know where he was driving *to*.
> *Bad*: Do you know *about* what the subject of the *Bhagavad Gita* is?
> *Better*: Do you know what the *Bhagavad Gita* is *about*?

In informal English usage, it is now acceptable to write and say:

Who is he going with?

In formal English usage, this question is:

With whom is he going?

Those grammarians who favor ending sentences with a preposition cite the famous quote by Winston Churchill, the 20th-century writer and politician. It appears in *Garner's Modern American English* and the *Chicago Manual of Style*, 16th edition, and is on many websites. When Churchill was criticized by a purist for ending a sentence with a preposition, he responded, "That is the type of arrant pedantry up with which I shall not put." I think Churchill's response puts this matter of whether to end a sentence with a preposition to rest.

3. *Prepositional idioms*: Many prepositions are used almost exclusively with certain words, creating a usage particular to American English. These idioms change frequently with popular usage. Check the Internet for a list of prepositional idioms. Use a current dictionary to check the idiom you select to use.

Be sure the idiom you select conveys the correct meaning of what you are saying. Note the difference in meaning in these two sentences below, though they both use *compared*.

Compared *with* Abbey's attendance, Jill's attendance is excellent. (to show difference)

Compared *to* others in the neighborhood, the D'Angelo family has the same size backyard. (to show similarities)

Conjunctions

Conjunctions are those important words in sentences that connect clauses, phrases, or words. Conjunctions create a relationship among those elements they connect. They do not change form and there are no comparisons for conjunctions. There are three main types of conjunctions that are discussed below.

Essentials

1. The coordinate conjunction is probably the most frequently used conjunction in writing.

A. Coordinate conjunctions connect elements that are related and equally important—they connect clauses to clauses, and phrases to phrases.

Quinlan attended the soccer game *and* then he went swimming.

B. Coordinate conjunctions connect words or groups of words that are the same kind: nouns to nouns, verbs to verbs, adjectives to adjectives, and adverbs to adverbs.

Quinlan *and* Dorothy attended the soccer game *and* then went to dinner.

C. There are seven coordinating conjunctions in English that establish a type of relationship between the words and phrases that these coordinating conjunctions connect. Those seven coordinating conjunctions and the relationships they create are *and* (addition), *but* (contrast), *for* (cause), *nor* (alternative), *or* (alternative), *so* (effect), and *yet* (contrast).

Hans can graduate in four years, *or*, in the accelerated program, in three years. (alternative)
The snow storm lasted only an hour, *but* dumped six inches of snow on the town. (contrast)
Keith ran the marathon in three hours, *so* he won a recognition medal. (effect)

2. Subordinate conjunctions connect clauses that are not equally important and cannot grammatically stand alone. Usually they connect an independent clause that has a subject and a verb and can stand alone to a clause that is "subordinate"—that is, a minor or a lower-ranked clause. Often the subordinate clause has a subject and verb, but it needs the independent clause to make sense.

Subordinate conjunctions never change form. Lists of the many subordinate conjunctions are on the Internet.

3. Correlative conjunctions are used in pairs. Some are coordinate conjunctions that team up with other words. There are eight common pairs of correlative conjunctions. These eight are listed on the next page along with the relationships they express.

as . . . as (comparison)
both . . . and (addition)
either . . . or (alternative)
neither . . . nor (negative)
not . . . but (substitution)
not only . . . but also (addition)
rather . . . than (alternative)
whether . . . or (alternative)

The Loner!

Interjections are a unique part of speech. They are not the nuts and bolts of a sentence—many a sentence has been written without interjections. They are an entity unto themselves. Usually they carry an exclamation point. See the punctuation chapter (chapter 1) for more about the exclamation point.

Interjections

According to Merriam-Webster Online, "an interjection is a word or phrase used in exclamation—a sudden utterance." Such words or phrases as *Yikes!* or *Dear me!* are interjections. Merriam-Webster goes on to say that when used in writing, interjections "usually do not have a grammatical connection." They do not describe words or connect words and phrases like the other parts of speech discussed in this chapter.

Check the punctuation chapter (chapter 1) for the section about exclamation points. Interjections usually take exclamation points.

Essentials

1. Swear words are interjections. In the 20th century the use of swear words in writing, particularly nonfiction, was discouraged. In the 21st century the standard has been relaxed. If you are writing papers for college classes, however, I caution you against using swear words in your papers.

2. There are no rules in grammar regarding interjections. However, do not overuse interjections in your writing. Interjections easily create a tone of extreme feeling, so use them sparingly.

Oh! I don't know the answer.
What! That's not possible.

One Last Word about Grammar

Now, perhaps, is a good time to remind you that grammar was not designed to confuse people. If you organize the eight parts of speech into four categories, the system of grammar is easier to discern. The foundation words or building blocks are the verbs, nouns, and pronouns. The describer words are adjectives and adverbs. The connectors are prepositions and conjunctions. And the loner part of speech is the interjection.

To be a better writer, start noticing sentences—their grammar and their punctuation. I recommend that you keep a digital file or an old-fashioned notebook of memorable sentences you have come across in your reading. Analyze the words in those sentences using the four categories as your basic guide. And, of course, review your own sentences. In the style and voice chapters, we will look at sentence construction again.

When reviewing grammar in your document, ask yourself:

1. Are there verbs in every sentence or do you punctuate fragments as sentences?

2. Are the verbs specific or are you only using a form of the verb *to be*?

3. Are the verbs the correct number (singular or plural) and tense?

4. Are you using many adjectives to describe the nouns in the sentences?

5. Do your pronouns refer to nouns?

6. Do adjectives only modify nouns or pronouns?

7. Do adverbs only modify verbs, adjectives, or adverbs?

8. In using comparisons of adjectives or adverbs, are you using the correct endings?

9. Are the coordinate conjunctions and correlative conjunctions used correctly?

10. Overall, are the foundation words in your sentences specific?

Practice

Below is a statement by the U.S. secretary of education about student loans in the United States. Read it over and identify what job each word in italics does in the designated sentences. On a separate sheet of paper, list letters A through G. From the list of words, select the correct job description and write it next to the corresponding letter.

noun	adjective	preposition
verb	adverb	conjunction
infinitive		

A. "Keeping *student* interest rates low is just part of our country's commitment to placing

B. a good education within reach for all who *are willing* to work for it. There is much

C. more work to do to bring *down* the cost of college, and all of us share responsibility

D. for ensuring that college is affordable for students *and* families around the country.

E. We look forward to continuing to work with *Congress* to figure out how we can

F. significantly bring down the overall debt that students and families have *to incur* to go

G. *to* college."

CHAPTER THREE
FACTS—THE ACCEPTABLE AND THE UNACCEPTABLE

Facts are hot items in the global 21st century. A fact, whether true or false, can electronically circle the world in a nanosecond. And facts can be manipulated and changed. It is even possible to alter primary sources. Photos can be changed using computer programs, and videos can be edited toward a particular slant or spin. In the 21st century it is more important than ever to constantly use your critical assessment skills in evaluating the facts you decide to cite in your writing.

Correct, vetted facts strengthen a piece and are essential to solid, creditable writing. Throughout history, all sorts of events have occurred based on so-called *facts* that had not been sufficiently vetted. When researching for a piece you are writing, be a skeptic. Learn to assess information, whether it is information you read in print or an e-book or information found on the Internet, a TV broadcast, or a video. You should recognize when an essay or speech or book or news report is advocating a point of view and whether the material you are reading cites questionable facts.

Essentials

1. False or misleading facts weaken any material, whether the material is nonfiction or a real-world event included in fiction. Facts, when used to bolster an opinion or argument, should be accurate, relevant, and effective in supporting the opinion.

2. Know the difference between primary and secondary sources. Use credible resources when citing primary and secondary sources. Verify facts by at least two sources that are either primary sources or secondary sources. Using primary sources to verify facts is usually the first choice of a writer, but credible secondary sources are just as acceptable.

3. Keep careful track of all the resources you consult. If you are using facts cited on a website, be sure you copy the website's URL and record the date on which you visited the website. Information on websites changes frequently as events evolve, so it is essential you cite the date that you accessed the website.

4. The Internet provides a wide variety of resources for gathering facts and checking facts. But be sure the websites you use in collecting facts and fact checking are reliable websites. Use your critical assessment skills in analyzing the credibility of a website.

5. Avoid plagiarism. Use appropriate documentation, and cite sources for facts and other people's ideas and interpretations that you include in your written piece.

6. Use trademarks only as adjectives and be sure to use correct spelling, capitalization, and punctuation.

What Are Facts?

Basically, facts are statements that can be verified by research. Do not confuse opinion with facts. The facts stated in these sentences can be verified.

> Rhode Island is the smallest state in the United States.
> The United States officially entered World War II on December 8, 1941.

Opinion:

> George Washington was a skillful general.
> Georgiana and Bill make a handsome couple.

Facts can employ statistics:

> According to the Bureau of Census of the United States, in the
> first year of the 21st century the estimated population was
> 285,669,915.

This sentence clearly describes the source for the statistic and describes the statistic as an estimate. It does not state the exact number of persons in the United States, which is an impossible number to arrive at.

When facts are used in support of a point of view or argument, facts should be relevant and connected to the point you are making. When researching, be sure to identify a fact from an opinion.

Researching Facts

Primary Sources

When researching and checking facts to use in your writing, look first for primary sources. As defined by the American Library Association, *primary sources* include all the records made at the time an event occurs—including electronic records such as e-mails. Memoirs and oral histories about an event, even though they are often written and recorded some time after an event occurs, are also primary sources.[1]

Basically in the 21st century we are awash in primary resources. Suppose you are doing research on the tragic events of September 11, 2001. Besides diaries, letters, speeches, newspapers, interviews, and journals, all of the photographs, videos, films, tape recordings, TV news reports, and website reports that were created when the United States was attacked by terrorists are primary sources for that event. In addition, the speeches and documents produced by the federal government, including Congress, the president's administration, and various departments such as the U.S. Department of State, Department of Defense, and Census Bureau, are primary source material. Legal documents, proclamations, and decrees are also primary source material.

And there is more—works of art made at the time of the event, including illustrations and paintings, poems, and music reflecting the event, are primary sources. Artifacts such as pieces of the World Trade Center's Twin Towers are primary sources for the events on September 11, 2001.

Secondary Sources

Materials created sometime after an event occurs that analyze or summarize that event are *secondary sources*. A book that analyzes the emergency response to the 9/11 terrorist attack on the United States is a secondary source. That book, though, may include primary resources such as speeches, e-mails, or letters written at the time of the attack.

Textbooks, encyclopedias, almanacs, dictionaries, nonfiction books analyzing almost any subject (history, literature, sociology, anthropology, etc.), and documentaries are secondary sources. Museum websites often have both primary and secondary sources. Government websites that provide histories and facts about various countries, such as the CIA World Factbook website, are considered secondary sources. When using secondary sources, make sure they are reliable and credible.

Researching on the Internet

The Internet is a vast tool for research. But it is important to use websites that are reliable and credible to research for facts. Just because information is on a website does not mean it is correct information. Use your critical assessment skills in analyzing the credibility of a website before using it as a reference. The American Library Association (see www.ala.org/rusa/resources/usingprimarysources) suggests asking questions about any website you are thinking of citing as a reference.[2] The questions basically include the following.

Source

1. Whose website is it? What is the name of the website and the organization that created the website? Is there a contact page for the organization? Is there a date given when the website was last updated?

2. Is the host of the website a credible organization? Did a library, university or college, or government create the website? Did a business create the website? The American Library Association lists six commonly known domain extensions (the last three letters of a web address) that you should be able to identify to help you assess the credibility of a website.

.edu	an educational institution
.gov	a U.S. government site
.org	organization or association
.museum	a museum
.com	a commercial site
.net	a personal or other site

3. What is the reason for the website? Is the website for research, or is it a website promoting a product or advocating an idea? Is there an "About" page on the website that gives background information about the organization the website represents? Is there a mission statement and a list of people who direct or work for the organization? Is an FAQ page available? Does the website have credible links that work?

Content

Carefully analyze the content of any website before using it as a reference.

1. Is the information on the website primary source material or secondary source material? If secondary source material, is the information quoted from cited sources?

2. Is there an author(s) cited for writing the information on the website? What are the credentials of the author(s)? Is the information well written and presented in a logical manner, or are there irrelevant facts and grammatical and punctuation errors?

3. If the information is secondary source material, such as an encyclopedia, has the information been vetted by a team of editors for accuracy? In the Digital Age, some encyclopedias are only vetted for accuracy by a group of volunteers. No board of professional, experienced editors checks and rechecks the facts provided in the entries of those encyclopedias. Many book publishers and academics find such secondary sources unacceptable.

Slant/Spin

Almost everything written today has a slant or spin. Use your critical assessment skills to identify the slant or spin of each website you are considering using as a resource.

1. Is the information biased and opinionated?

2. Does the information exaggerate facts or express extreme anger or hate?

3. If a point of view is expressed, is that view supported with credible facts?

4. Are there legitimate sources cited for the facts mentioned on the website?

Design

Look at the overall design of the website.

1. Is the website designed to enable easy access to various pages of the website?

2. Does the website have more bells and whistles than content?

3. Are there many commercial ads on the website and other distracting elements?

The American Library Association also suggests you learn more about the website itself. Google the website you might use and see if any credible organization has reviewed the site and the information on the website.

Libraries and the Internet

Most libraries subscribe to various Internet subscription archive programs that can be used on computers at the library. Many libraries make a number of these Internet subscription research programs available for free. The usual requirement is for a user to have a library card and register to use the Internet subscription research programs. It is possible to do a great amount of Internet research accessing library data programs from your computer regardless of where you are located.

When I was researching a family that lived in Washington, DC, in 1884, I was able to access, using my home computer, the actual census page of 1880 listing the family. The information included their address, the names and number of children and their ages (so I could figure out their birth dates), and the names, ages, and occupations of adults in the home. I could even print out that page. I did this through a library for which I had a library card and was registered to use its Internet data programs. The entire search took me approximately five minutes.

Appropriate Websites

Use websites that are appropriate and credible resource sites for your work. If you are writing a nonfiction piece about the history of the United States in the Korean War, for instance, what primary source websites and secondary source websites would be appropriate to use? Below is a sample list of primary and secondary sources for various topics.

Researching the United States in the Korean War

The United States fought the Korean War from 1950 to 1953. Many primary sources and important secondary sources are available on credible websites.

Finding Primary Sources: The United States in the Korean War

1. Access presidential libraries of Harry S. Truman and Dwight D. Eisenhower, both presidents during the Korean War.

2. Research U.S. government archives at the U.S. National Archives. These would be a source of information for war casualties, for example.

3. Access the U.S. *Congressional Record* and search for congressional speeches and reports about the Korean War.

4. Search for Korean War photos at the Library of Congress digital "Print and Photograph" website.

5. Research the archives websites of American newspapers that cover international and national events such as the *New York Times* and *Washington Post.*

6. Check the archives of newspapers throughout the world for a global perspective of the United States in the Korean War. Some foreign newspapers have English editions.

7. Access the archives of international organizations involved in the Korean War such as the United Nations.

8. Search the web for any diaries or memoirs by soldiers who fought in the Korean War. Remember, however, that these diaries or memoirs are personal interpretations of events and have not been vetted.

Finding Secondary Sources: The United States in the Korean War

1. Research U.S. government websites such as the Department of State, the Department of Defense, and the Central Intelligence Agency for web pages about the Korean War. Some of the material might be primary source documents; some of the material might be a history of the Korean War (from a U.S. government view), which would be a secondary source.

2. Check your school or municipal library for history books about the Korean War.

3. Access vetted encyclopedias, which are usually available free through the database of your college or town library.

4. Search for magazines and journals that have published articles discussing the events that occurred in the Korean War.

Researching the Life of Elvis Presley

Whatever the subject you are researching, you have a variety of choices to use, as shown in the list of sources for researching the life of Elvis Presley.

Finding Primary Sources: The Life of Elvis Presley

Elvis Presley never wrote a memoir about his life or music, but there are still many primary resources available for researching his life.

1. Use the Internet to search for primary source documents about Presley, such as his birth certificate, marriage license, and death certificate.

2. Access newspaper, magazine, and journal accounts written by people who attended events in Presley's life, such as when he reported for duty to the U.S. Army in 1958, or such events as his public performances throughout the United States.

3. Research the music division of the Library of Congress for first-hand accounts about rock 'n' roll and specifically Presley's music.

4. Access websites of various rock 'n' roll museums.

5. Check libraries and book outlets for memoirs by rock 'n' roll stars and others who knew Elvis Presley throughout his life.

Finding Secondary Sources: The Life of Elvis Presley

1. Check libraries and bookstores for books written about Elvis Presley.

2. Access vetted encyclopedias, which are usually available free through the database of your college or town library.

3. Search newspaper and magazine articles about Elvis Presley.

4. Read the official biography on the Elvis Presley website. Remember that this appears on the *official* Presley website and presents information with a slant to promote Elvis Presley.

5. Research Presley's fan clubs and assess the biographical information they have about Presley.

Researching the Hubble Space Telescope

Be aware of the numerous government websites that have primary source and secondary source material for such items as the Hubble Space Telescope.

CHAPTER THREE

Finding Primary Sources: The Hubble Space Telescope

1. Research NASA and other government agencies' websites for the history, facts, current news, and photos of the Hubble Space Telescope. Also investigate online and print records of presidential and congressional speeches and statements made about the Hubble Space Telescope.

2. Investigate coverage by news outlets online, in print, and on TV reporting events involving the Hubble Space Telescope.

3. Check museums such as the Smithsonian and libraries such as the Library of Congress for primary source material about the Hubble Space Telescope.

4. Look for diaries, letters, or articles written by astronomer Edwin Powell Hubble, the namesake of the Hubble Space Telescope.

5. Look for diaries or letters on the Internet written by team members who worked on launching the telescope and workers who now monitor the telescope.

Finding Secondary Sources: The Hubble Space Telescope

1. Check encyclopedias online and print for information about the Hubble Space Telescope.

2. Look for books, magazine articles, and websites that analyze the Hubble Space Telescope's successes and failures and its contributions to knowledge about outer space.

3. Search for information about the life of astronomer Edwin Powell Hubble in print books and credible online websites.

Researching the Founding of Google, Inc.

Google, Inc., is often called one of the most successful Internet companies in the Digital Age, and in its short history there are many primary and secondary sources discussing the company's founding in the late 20th century.

Finding Primary Sources: The Founding of Google, Inc.

1. Check the website of Google, Inc., for an "About" page or company history page. Remember that this information is written by the company and probably is only positive about the company.

2. Look for interviews of Google, Inc., founders Larry Page and Sergey Bin in magazines, in newspapers, and on TV news outlets. Check also for memoirs or blogs written by Larry Page or Sergey Bin.

3. Search museums such as the Computer History Museum. Be sure to review the members on the museum's Board of Directors. Are most of the members affiliated with computer companies? Do you think the museum has an interest in presenting all the positives about computers rather than the negatives?

4. Research the Library of Congress and other government websites for primary source documents regarding Google, Inc.

Finding Secondary Sources: The Founding of Google, Inc.

1. Check vetted encyclopedias for entries about Google, Inc., or the founders Larry Page and Sergey Bin.

2. Review library catalogs for print and e-books written about Google or its two founders. Look especially for those books that include Google's start-up history, including its early successes and challenges.

3. Look for magazine, journal, and newspaper articles, including editorials and blogs that analyze the events leading to Google's founding.

Citing Resources

When citing sources used in your writing, select a style book and follow that style consistently. Many writers and students use the most recently published *Chicago Manual of Style*. It has an extensive section on how to style resource citations for footnotes, endnotes, or notes within the text.

The citation examples include books, magazines, newspapers, speeches, interviews, laws, and all manner of electronic publications—even e-mails. The manual is available online for a subscription fee and in a print edition.

If you are a graduate student working in a specialized area of expertise, learn the stylebook of your specialized field. The American Psychological Association has its own stylebook, *APA Publication Manual*, which is used by writers, students, and publications in the social sciences. The Modern Language Association has two stylebooks, the *MLA Style Manual* and the *MLA Style Manual and Guide to Scholarly Publishing*. Both are often used for academic papers and publications. These manuals also cite examples of how to style footnotes, endnotes, or notes within the text. Professors usually tell their students which style book to use for citations in assigned class papers, and publishers tell writers which style book to use for citations in their contracted manuscripts.

Keeping Track of Resources

It is essential that you keep track of the resources you consult and use in your writing. For tracking websites, include the title of the website, subject, URL, and date(s) you accessed each website. The *MLA Handbook for Writers of Research Papers* suggests you put your research into one of three types of records: a record of exact wording you copy from a resource with citations, a record of your summary of resources you have read along with citations, and a record of your ideas about the subject of your writing.[3]

Copyright

The first bit of information you should know and remember about copyright is that in the United States everything you create—write down or create in a word-processing program or on a blog—is protected by copyright. Your diary is copyrighted—even though you probably have not registered it with the U.S. Copyright Office. Your diary is protected by what is called common law copyright. The U.S. copyright law covers all "original works of authorship" that the copyright law says "are fixed in a tangible form of expression." Writing in a diary, writing online—these are all "a tangible form of expression."

This means that if you use a quote from a blog in your writing, you have to cite that blog. The blog might not carry a copyright line at the bottom of its website pages, but the content on the blog is still protected by copyright.

Copyright covers a broad range of work, including literary, musical, dramatic, pictorial, graphic, architectural, and sculptural works; computer websites; motion pictures; and sound recordings. The music industry, for example, has won major copyright litigation against people who have pirated copyrighted music on the Internet. There is one significant limitation of the author's rights under the copyright law, and that is the "doctrine of fair use." See the section below that discusses fair use.

The Protections of a U.S. Copyright

The United States has a long history of copyright protection that reaches back to 1783, when the Continental Congress governed. Not having the power to pass a federal copyright law, the Continental Congress passed a resolution recommending to the states that they pass legislation protecting the rights of authors for a term not less than 14 years. Of the 15 states at the time, all but Delaware heeded the Congress and passed copyright laws.

In Article 1, Section 8, the U.S. Constitution ratified in 1787 gave Congress the right to secure exclusive rights of authors and inventors to their work for a limited time. In 1790, Congress passed the first federal copyright law that secured the rights of writers and inventors for a term not less than 14 years. Successor copyright laws have followed into the 21st century.

Today, the current U.S. copyright law was passed in 1976 and new laws have been passed to add to the 1976 copyright law to cover works in the Digital Age. The 1976 law basically covers works written after January 1, 1978, from the time the work was created through the author's life, plus 70 years after the author's death. Works written before January 1, 1978, now are covered for the same period as works written after January 1, 1978. Remember that a copyright protects a work regardless of whether the author formally registers the work with the U.S. Copyright Office.

One law passed by Congress to cover copyrights of digital and computer works is the No Electronic Theft Act (NET) passed in 1997. It covers prosecuting those who violate copyrights on Internet websites. The act makes it a federal crime to copy, distribute, or share copies of electronic copyrighted materials on websites even if your sharing is for no commercial purposes and even if you receive no financial remuneration for the material. This particularly speaks to making Internet copyrighted materials available on computer networks.

Registering Your Work

There are benefits for registering your writing, even if unpublished, with the U.S. Copyright Office. Registration creates a public record of the copyright. Before any lawsuit claiming infringement of copyright can be filed, a work must be registered.

Registering a work takes three steps. You must file an application form, pay a nonreturnable fee, and make a nonreturnable deposit to the copyright office of the work you are registering. You can file online. For further information, visit the U.S. Copyright Office website.

U.S. Copyright and Other Nations

In this global world, it is good to know something about U.S. copyright agreements with other nations. The U.S. Office of Copyright cautions that an "international copyright" that protects an author's work throughout the world does not exist. In Circular 38A, the Office of Copyright points out that copyright protection in a particular foreign country depends on that country's national copyright laws. Since the agreements of numerous countries to various international copyright conventions and treaties, many countries offer some sort of protection to foreign works. These treaties and conventions include the historic Berne Convention, which dates back to 1886 and was last updated in 1979, and the more recent World Trade Organization's Agreement on Trade-Related Aspects of Intellectual Property Rights, which the United States agreed to in 2005. For more information about U.S. copyright and international conventions and treaties, check Circular 38A issued by the U.S. Office of Copyright.

Fair Use under U.S. Copyrights

The owners of copyrights do have a limitation to their rights. This limitation means that their copyrighted materials can be used or reproduced without the copyright holders giving permission. The 1976 Copyright Law calls such usage the "fair use" of text.

Section 107 of the 1976 copyright law is titled "Limitations on Exclusive Rights: Fair Use." This section creates an important limitation on the copyright holder and enables authors to use a limited amount of copyrighted material, naturally citing the source of the material, without obtaining permission from the author of the quoted material.

Though Section 107 does not precisely enumerate limitations of fair use, it does list factors that should be considered when deciding whether use of copyrighted material is fair. These factors listed in Section 107 are as follows:

1. The purpose and character of the use, including whether such use is of commercial nature or is for nonprofit educational purposes

2. The nature of the copyrighted work

3. The amount and substantiality of the portion used in relation to the copyrighted work as a whole

4. The effect of the use upon the potential market for, or value of, the copyrighted work

If in your writing you are going to quote from an author's work under the fair use doctrine, be sure the quote appears correctly, attribute it to the author, and do not quote out of context. Publishers often establish their own rules regarding fair use, usually citing a specific number of words that can be considered fair use. But such rules do not apply to copyright infringement cases. Remember, fair use, if questioned by the quoted author, is decided by the courts. Given that there is no clear definition of fair use, it is wise to be cautious when using the doctrine of fair use.

Plagiarism

According to the Merriam-Webster Online dictionary, *to plagiarize* is a transitive verb that means "to steal and pass off [the ideas or words of another] as one's own; use [another's production] without crediting the source." In other words, it means to use an organization or person's work as your own and not credit that person or organization.

Resources such as the *ALA Manual* and the *ALA Manual and Guide to Scholarly Publishing* point out that plagiarism is an ethical issue, not a copyright legal issue. In the 21st century, academics, writers, and students have much to lose if they plagiarize. There are cases of academics losing their jobs, writers losing contracts, and students being expelled from college for plagiarizing. Whatever you plagiarize, regardless of the writing, it will reflect negatively on your reputation, your work, and your studies.[4]

The Yale College Writing Center (at http://writing.yalecollege.yale.edu/what-plagiarism) states, "You must always make clear in your written work where you have borrowed from others—whether data, opinions, questions, ideas, or specific language."[5] This sage piece of advice also applies to any speeches, lectures, or graphics—such as charts and graphs.

Essentials

1. Plagiarism occurs when you purposefully use the exact words of already published or spoken material, but do not cite the source of those words you are using, in your writing (including your blogs on the Internet), speech, or lecture.

2. If you use someone else's spoken or written words, ideas, or theories but you put those original words, ideas, and theories in your own words, you still must cite your sources of the original work. Otherwise, you are plagiarizing.

3. Even if you use quotation marks to show you are using a direct quote, you have to cite the source.

4. Your sources must be cited for any information you use that is not *common knowledge*.

Defining Common Knowledge

As the Yale Writing Center points out, the definition of *common knowledge* is "ambiguous."[6] Broadly, the term means knowledge that is known by most people. That is difficult to define precisely, so it is up to your astute judgment to review the facts and ideas in your writing and decide whether they need attribution or fall into the category of common knowledge.

Facts such as *Terrorists attacked the United States on September 11, 2001* or *Thomas Jefferson was the third president of the United States* could be used without citation. Even if you had to look up these facts in a reference book, these facts are considered common knowledge. But be cautious in calling all the facts used in your writing common knowledge.

Be especially careful about opinions expressed in your writing. Are they your own or did you read them on a website or in a book? Again, if the opinion falls into the general opinion category that most people know, then it is common knowledge. An example of a common knowledge opinion is this: *Apple is a very successful computer company.*

But the more specific your subject, the less the chance that the facts and opinions you include in your writing will fall into the common knowledge category. If, for example, you are writing a specific history about what happened in Japanese schools during World War II, a sentence that states "*One first-grade textbook of the time begins with the words 'Forward March, Forward March, Soldiers, Forward March.'*" needs attribution. The sentence is from the book *Japan: A Historical Survey* by Mikiso Hane, which was published in 1972. The more specific the subject you are writing about, the fewer facts and opinions would fall into the common knowledge category.

Remember, it is better to include citations for facts you think the average person would not know than to risk plagiarism.

Examples of Plagiarism

Below is a quote from the *History of the Decline and Fall of the Roman Empire* by Edward Gibbon. The quote is Gibbon's description of the Roman Empire in the second century CE. The wording and the assessment—the ideas expressed here about the Empire—are Gibbon's original work, and if used, the source must be cited even though the six volumes were first published between 1776 and 1788.

> In the second century of the Christian Aera [era], the empire of Rome comprehended the fairest part of the earth, and the most civilized portion of mankind. The frontiers of that extensive monarchy were guarded

by ancient renown and disciplined valor. The gentle but powerful influence of laws and manners had gradually cemented the union of the provinces. Their peaceful inhabitants enjoyed and abused the advantages of wealth and luxury. The image of a free constitution was preserved with decent reverence: the Roman senate appeared to possess the sovereign authority, and devolved on the emperors all the executive powers of government.[7]

Below is a paragraph that plagiarizes this quote. The words in italics are words and phrases that use Gibbon's precise wording without using quotation marks or crediting the author.

In the second century of the Common Era, the Roman Empire was the most *civilized portion* of the known world. The frontiers of the Empire were guarded by a *disciplined valor.* The *powerful influence of laws and manners* had gradually united the provinces. The inhabitants *enjoyed and abused the advantages of wealth and luxury.* The *free constitution was preserved with decent reverence and the Roman senate possessed the sovereign authority* and delegated to *the emperors the executive powers of government.*

Below is an example of plagiarism using some of Gibbon's words in paraphrasing and using Gibbon's *ideas* about the Empire without attributing them to the author.

The Roman Empire in the second century, Common Era, was the *fairest a*nd most *civilized* area of the world. The frontiers were guarded by *disciplined valor* and the *influence of laws had united* the provinces. The people *enjoyed and often abused* the *advantages wealth and luxury* bring.

If you are writing about the Roman Empire and want to give your readers a picture of what the Empire was like in the second century, Gibbon's book is a good source. But to use any part of his assessment of the Empire, you have to credit Edward Gibbon and his book, *History of the Decline and Fall of the Roman Empire.* The passage below correctly cites Edward Gibbon's words and ideas from his book.

In his book *History of the Decline and Fall of the Roman Empire,* Edward Gibbon describes the Roman Empire in the second century of the

Common Era as "the fairest part of the earth, and the most civilized portion of mankind." Gibbon explains that the frontiers of the Empire were "guarded by ancient renown and disciplined valor." According to Gibbon, the "powerful influence of laws and manners" had united the provinces. The people of the provinces "enjoyed and abused" the advantages of a wealthy Empire.

Citing Vague Sources

Be specific when you cite resources, and avoid vague references. If you read a document that often cites an "unnamed government official," a phrase commonly used in the early years of the 21st century, question that. Ask yourself if the author of the document deliberately and knowingly used such a vague reference. I call this deliberate obscurity. Avoid using resources with such citations, and avoid using that phrase in your writing.

Fabrication

Be aware of fabrication by newspapers and on websites of events and news. In the 21st century, news reports and facts in reporters' columns have been fabricated. Fabrication has occurred even in the *New York Times*. Note that fabrication is one of the pitfalls of the Digital Age.

Trademarks

We live in a commercial culture and a litigious society. Any writing in the 21st century must include careful attention to using trademarks correctly. Product and corporation trademarks are assiduously protected. Because branding is an important aspect of marketing products, corporations often bring a lawsuit against a trademark violation, especially if the misused trademark appears in print or online in a for-profit publication.

Essentials

1. According to the Merriam-Webster Online dictionary, a trademark is a word that points distinctly to the "origin or ownership of merchandise to which it is applied and legally reserved

to the exclusive use of the owner as maker or seller." Trademarks help a business to build a brand for products or services it sells.

2. The spelling, punctuation, capitalization, and design of a product or corporate name are all part of the trademark.

3. Trademarks are marked with either ® or ™ after the name. The ™ indicates that the word or name is in the process of becoming a registered trademark and is protected. The ® indicates the word or name is a registered trademark.

Do not confuse trademarks with a copyright or a patent.

> *Trademarks* protect words, phrases, symbols, or designs identifying products or services of one corporation or business or organization.
> *Copyrights* protect authored, original works—books, plays, poems, texts, and songs.
> *Patents* protect inventions or discoveries.

Trademark Violations

What is considered a trademark violation? Trademark violations occur when a trademark is misused or misspelled in print or on screen (including videos). If you write a blog about burger empires and misspell McDonald's, the McDonald's Corporation can legally bring a lawsuit. The McDonald's Corporation owns the word *McDonald's* spelled exactly as it appears here. If in reference to the burger empire you do not use the apostrophe, that is a misspelling of the trademark.

Checking Trademarks

International Trademark Association

Although individual countries award trademarks, the International Trademark Association located in New York City keeps track of trademarks worldwide. The Association is a good source for checking the correct spelling and punctuation of trademarks.

International Trademark Association

    Website: http://www.inta.org

    Checklist: http://www.inta.org/Media/Pages/TrademarkChecklist.aspx

    E-mail: tmhotline@inta.org. Send an e-mail that includes a brief description of the trademark(s) in question. For a list of trademarks, e-mail at least two weeks before your deadline.

Corporate Website

    Check a corporation's website to see what products and names are trademarks. Most corporate websites have a "Terms of Use" page in which corporate trademarks are listed. The Terms of Use page also provides information about how the trademark(s) can legally be used. Corporations carefully protect their trademarks and keep these pages updated.

    Google the product name and find the corporate website for the product. Notice how the corporation uses the product name in its website text. Be sure to check the masthead of the website to see if one of the trademark indications (® or ™) is used.

Dictionaries

    American English dictionaries often indicate whether a word or name is a trademark. Words such as *Kleenex, Dumpster, Xerox, Styrofoam*, and *Levi's* are on Merriam-Webster Online. But dictionaries do not include all trademarks. A random search of Merriam-Webster Online found that the following trademarks were not in the dictionary: *Microsoft, iPhone, Apple*, and *iPod*.

Trademarks in Texts

    Often in a book, a reference to trademarks used in the text will appear on the copyright page, such as the following: "Every effort to identify trademarks has been made. Trademarks are indicated by their correct spelling and capitalization." Sometimes the publisher will list the trademarks on the copyright page with the appropriate trademark indicated.

    Fortunately, most book publishers are not interrupting text with a ® or a ™ mark in print or e-books. But because branding is becoming such a worldwide corporate goal, it is perhaps only a matter of time before these marks enter the text of both nonfiction and fiction books.

On websites and in news releases I have seen trademark indicators appear the first time the trademark appears in the text, then they are left off in other references to the specific trademark. Always include the names of trademarks on the Style Sheet you make for each document you write. (For more on Style Sheets, see chapter 6.)

Using Trademarks

Basically words such as *Pepsi*, *Kleenex*, *Levi's*, and *Xerox* are trademarks and need to be capped and written according to their trademarked style when appearing in print and online text. It is important that all references to a trademark in a document be accurate and consistent. For example, *Levi's* always has an apostrophe and *KitchenAid* is always spelled as one word and with a capital A.

The International Trademark Association Guidelines point out that some trademarks get lost. The words are so frequently misused by the writing public and the corporations owning the trademarks do little to stop that misuse, so the words lose their trademark status. Once, words such as *aspirin*, *elevator*, *corn flakes*, and *yo-yo* were famous trademarks, capped and with rights exclusively owned by a company. Today, due to misuse of the marks (general public misuse in print), they are merely generic product names in most nations of the world. However, do note that the term *Bayer Aspirin* is a registered trademark that is owned and protected by the Bayer Company, and it is capped.

Because some brands lose their trademark status, the International Trademark Association stresses that trademarks and service marks should only be used as proper adjectives. Do not use trademarks as nouns or verbs. Always use trademarks as adjectives before generic nouns that define the product. Examples from the guidelines of the International Trademark Association include the following:

Correct: The boss bought a Xerox brand copier.
Wrong: I am going to Xerox these copies.
Correct: Please hand me a Kleenex tissue.
Wrong: It was a five-Kleenex movie.
Correct: Send the packages via FedEx courier.
Wrong: Send the packages via FedEx.

Correct: I had four Starbucks lattes at the beach.
Wrong: I drank four Starbucks at the beach.

When using trademarks correctly, as proper adjectives, you should not use the possessive or plural form—unless the trademark includes a plural or possessive form. Examples include *Levi's* and *McDonald's*. Do not use trademarks that include a possessive as a double possessive.

Wrong: The McDonald's' burgers are known worldwide.
Correct: The burgers sold by McDonald's are known worldwide.

Start correctly identifying trademarks! Which is it? HomeDepot or The Home Depot; K-mart or Kmart or K-Mart? (The correct trademarks are: The Home Depot; Kmart.)

For an in-depth discussion of trademarks, go to the International Trademark Association's booklet, "A Guide to Proper Trademark Use," at http://www.inta.org/Media/Documents/2011_TMUseMediaInternet Publishing.pdf.

One Last Word

The Digital Age provides access to many primary sources, but it also enables primary sources, such as photo images, to be altered. When researching a subject, be extra careful to critically analyze both primary and secondary sources. This particularly includes websites. Avoid plagiarism. In researching, take careful notes so that you can correctly attribute exact quotes, paraphrases, and ideas to their sources. Remember: Critical thinking skills are especially important in the Digital Age.

When the piece you are researching and writing is finished, give it one last check for the items discussed in this chapter.

1. Check that the facts you cite are relevant and correct. Make sure your sources are credible and correct and you did not plagiarize your sources.

2. Make sure your citations follow a recognized style book.

3. Be sure the spelling, punctuation, and capitalization of all proper nouns are correct. This includes names of people, organizations, places, and trademarks.

4. Check that your references to dates, time, and seasons are correct.

5. Check any citations of statistics, including your sources for the statistics.

6. Look for any exaggerated statements you might have made in the piece without citing any relevant, credible facts. Look to tone down those statements.

Practice

Can you identify plagiarism? A student used for information the paragraphs quoted below from "Amplified Greenhouse Effect Shifts North's Growing Seasons" by Kathryn Hansen on NASA's Science website.

Information

"Vegetation growth at Earth's northern latitudes increasingly resembles lusher latitudes to the south, according to a NASA-funded study based on a 30-year record of ground-based and satellite data sets.

"[A]n international team of university and NASA scientists examined the relationship between changes in surface temperature and vegetation growth from 45 degrees north latitude to the Arctic Ocean. Results show temperature and growth at northern latitudes now resemble those found 4 degrees to 6 degrees of latitude farther south as recently as 1982. . . .

"As a result of enhanced warming and a longer growing season, large patches of vigorously productive vegetation now span a third of the northern landscape, or more than 3.5 million square miles (9 million square kilometers). That is an area about equal to the contiguous United States."

Student Paper

The paper that the student wrote about global warming is below. On a separate sheet of paper, list the ideas, words, and phrases you think are examples of plagiarism.

A.   Using a 30-year record of satellite data sets, a global team of university and NASA scientists recently evaluated the connection between the

B.   growth of vegetation and surface temperature in the world. They studied an area from the 45 degree north latitude, which runs through the U.S. states of Maine, Minnesota, South Dakota, Idaho, and Oregon, to the 70 degree north latitude, the beginning of the Arctic Ocean.

    The study reveals that both temperature and vegetation growth between the two latitudes have changed and now they are similar to those found at the 38 to 41 degrees north latitudes 30 years ago. The scientists claim that the growing season in the area studied is longer and the temperatures are warmer. As a result large swaths of vegetation

C.   now cover the northern landscape. They estimate that vegetation now

D.   covers an area of over 3.5 million square miles or an area about equal to the contiguous United States.

E.   (Overall, does the author give any attribution?)

Notes

1. American Library Association, "Using Primary Sources on the Web," accessed July 25, 2013, http://www.ala.org/rusa/resources/usingprimarysources.

2. American Library Association, "Evaluating Primary Source Web Sites," accessed July 25, 2013, http://www.ala.org/rusa/sections/history/resources/pubs/usingprimarysources#evaluating.

3. Modern Language Association of America, *MLA Handbook for Writers of Research Papers*, 7th ed. (New York: Modern Language Association of America, 2009), 61.

4. Modern Language Association of America, *A Manual and Guide to Scholarly Publishing*, 3rd ed. (New York: Modern Language Association of America, 2008), 166.

5. Yale College Writing Center, "What Is Plagiarism?" accessed July 25, 2013, http://writing.yalecollege.yale.edu/what-plagiarism.

6. Yale College Writing Center, "Common Knowledge," accessed July 26, 2013, http://writing.yalecollege.yale.edu/common-knowledge.

7. Edward Gibbon, *History of the Decline and Fall of the Roman Empire*, 6 vols., 1776–1788, accessed September 12, 2013, Gutenberg.org/files/731/731-h/731-h.htm#link2HCH0001.

CHAPTER FOUR
STYLE—CREATE UNIQUE WRITING

The style of a piece includes the mechanics and essential content—its substance. The mechanics of a written piece are its spelling, punctuation, capitalization, and grammar. The mechanics subtly affect the rhythm and pace of a written piece. The content—what is said and how it is said—determines the tone and the flow of a document. Style, then, is the relationship between the mechanics and the content. Your writing style is the way you blend the mechanics with the substance of your writing.

You should adopt the habit of noticing style in what you read. This is especially easy to do if you read news reports online. Consider these two opening paragraphs for Norman Borlaug's obituary, which recently appeared online. Norman Borlaug's work had an enormous influence on the world, but he is not well known.

> Associated Press: "Agricultural scientist Norman Borlaug, the father of the 'green revolution' who won the Nobel Peace Prize for his role in combating world hunger and saving hundreds of millions of lives, died Saturday in Texas, a Texas A&M University spokeswoman said. He was 95."[1]
>
> *New York Times*: "Norman E. Borlaug, the plant scientist who did more than anyone else in the 20th century to teach the world to feed itself and whose work was credited with saving hundreds of millions of lives, died Saturday night. He was 95 and lived in Dallas."[2]

Which opening has the better style? Let's first look at the mechanics. The AP refers immediately to the green revolution, which it puts in quotes. Words in quotes alert readers—what is this alert about? Is the term not legitimate, or is it a reference to the go-green slogans of the 21st century?

Consider the substance and content of the paragraphs. The AP uses the term *agricultural scientist*. What exactly does that mean? The *New York Times* states Borlaug was a *plant scientist*—a specific term that tells me he worked with plants—and that he did outstanding work in the 20th century, which places him in history. I don't need to know who announced his death, as the AP states. I need specific information about what Borlaug did and why he is famous.

For an opener, the *New York Times* has a better style; it is clear and concise. The mechanics in the opening paragraph are not confusing. The content and substance tell me what I need to know. Overall, the opening paragraph flows well.

In this chapter we will discuss the age-old and current advice about creating a writing style. We will examine specific mechanics and consider what creates tone and flow in substance that contribute to a style.

Essentials

1. The conventional advice about creating a style is to aim for clarity.

2. Keep the mechanics in the piece consistent within each document.

3. Write an outline that structures the document you are going to write.

4. Use specific language in presenting relevant and reliable facts.

5. Learn to recognize characteristics of style in your writing and in what you read.

Clarity

In the West, the first discussion about style is attributed to the ancient Greeks. Sometime in the third century BCE, Aristotle wrote *Rhetoric,* in which he talks about the art of speaking and writing. He also wrote *Poetics*, which we will look at in chapter 5. His discussion in *Rhetoric* is especially good to read for advice about style. And although Aristotle gives advice to both speakers and writers (in ancient Greece, oratory was considered an art form), his advice about language usage is still repeated in the 21st century.

> Style to be good must be clear. . . . Clearness is secured by using the words (nouns and verbs alike) that are current and ordinary. . . . Strange words, compound words, and invented words must be used sparingly.[3]

Compare Aristotle's suggestions with the advice in a modern classic, Strunk and White's *Elements of Style*. Many of the 21 items in its "List of Reminders" are similar to Aristotle's advice: "(2) Write in a way that comes naturally," "(4) Write with nouns and verbs," "(14) Avoid fancy words," and "(16) Be clear."[4]

As for Professor Strunk's advice to "omit needless words" (rule 17), that is also discussed by Aristotle in his statement that "the foundation of good style is correctness of language," and the second "correctness" that he lists is "call[ing] things by their own special names and not by vague general ones." And Aristotle further urges "avoid[ing] ambiguities" in prose.[5]

As you can see, the discussion of clarity issues has continued for eons. The discussion particularly heated up in the 20th century in reaction to the Victorian Age writing style. Note that the first edition of *Elements of Style*, privately printed by Professor Strunk for Cornell University students, appeared in 1918. English in 1918, even American English, still felt the effects of Victorian Age writing. Writers of the Victorian Age might have thought they wrote with clarity and simplicity, but to many American writers in the early 20th century, brevity was long overdue. Even poets rebelled against Victorian Age poetry. In the early 20th century, American Imagist poets like William Carlos Williams, Amy Lowell, and Ezra Pound wrote and published succinct, brief poems in contrast to wordy Victorian poetry.

Besides *Elements of Style*, other writing books appeared in the 20th century such as William Zinsser's *Writing Well*. The message was the same—write with clarity and simplicity.

This discussion and advice about style continue into the 21st century. If you look in any contemporary guide to good writing, you will find similar advice: Write with *clarity* and write *naturally*.

The new wrinkle to this age-old advice is the Internet, which daily affects style in written English whether it is in print or online. Strunk and White and Zinsser wrote their books before the age of the computer, although in Zinsser's last update of his book he included using word processing to write. Just what effect the computer—writing using a keyboard and screen with built-in ease for making changes and corrections—has had on writing style is difficult to precisely measure. But the computer is changing English language usage, just as in the past all technological advances for recording the written word changed language usage.

When writing for a web page on the Internet, we have all sorts of choices regarding the presentation of text. Do we create a bulleted list enumerating the major content of the text? Do we include many links to other websites that further explain cited facts or illustrate points made in the text?

These choices do include issues of mechanics as well as substance, and they do affect style. If we enumerate our content in bulleted lists, we might fail to explore the complexities of the content. Inserting many links can cause too many distractions for the reader. The Digital Age is both a challenge to conventional American English and a time of great excitement as American English adopts and adapts to new technology.

Mechanics

When we talk about the mechanics of writing, we are talking about the word details in a written piece: capitalization, contractions, grammar, number style, punctuation, and the citation of any facts included in a written piece. It is essential that you decide on a style of these details and follow that style throughout each document you write. In short, keep the mechanics consistent.

Many writers make a Style Sheet as they write, noting what words they capitalize, whether they use contractions, and the grammar—particularly whether they use the active voice, the passive voice, or both verb voices. They note on their Style Sheets the number style—whether numbers are digits or spelled out—as well as the punctuation style and what style book they use for citing facts. Style Sheets are discussed further in chapter 6. Below is a discussion of each mechanical detail. Familiarize yourself with these mechanics.

Capitalization

You must consistently capitalize proper nouns used in your document. Place names are proper nouns: New York City; Des Moines, Iowa; and Kansas City, Missouri. But what about the other nouns that you are unsure whether to capitalize? Do you know, for example, the correct capitalization of the vegetable *brussels sprouts* or the flower called *jack-in-the-pulpit*? Are both terms capitalized? When you write "The sun set beautifully in the *western* sky," do you capitalize *western*? Or if you write "Charles went *west* after he graduated from the University of Maryland," is *west* capitalized? What about computer terms? If you write "To research her ancestry, Gertrude used the *Internet* to go to the National Archives *web* page," do you capitalize *Internet* but not *web*?

To answer these questions, turn to reference works. An online dictionary is a good source for checking the capitalization of nouns. A style book, such as the most recent edition of the *Chicago Manual of Style*, also will answer questions about capitalization.

FYI: Brussels sprouts and jack-in-the-pulpit are in the dictionary. The former takes a capital B for Brussels; the latter is a common noun. Per *Chicago Manual of Style*, 16th edition, the phrase *western sky* should not have a capital *w*, as here the word *western* is used as an adjective. In the phrase *went West*, the *W* should be capitalized, for *West* is used to designate a major geographical area. The word *Internet* is capitalized in both Merriam-Webster Online and the *Chicago Manual of Style*. The word *web* is now lowercased when used generically, per *Chicago Manual of Style*, 16th edition. In American English, the capitalization of words changes over time!

An example of capitalization changing is the term *website*. For years, the *Chicago Manual of Style* and the Merriam-Webster Online dictionary called for the term to be written as *Web site*. But popular usage insisted on spelling the term as one word in the lowercase: *website*. Now, the 16th edition of the *Chicago Manual of Style* has bowed to popular usage and styles the term as *website*. Merriam-Webster Online, as of this writing, still styles the term as *Web site*.

What do you do when the references differ on capitalization? If there is disagreement in the reputable dictionary and style guide you consult, make a choice, and be consistent in using what style you choose. This is where a Style Sheet really is a valuable tool in helping to keep the details of a document's mechanics consistent. In the vocabulary section of your Style Sheet, list the words you capitalize or words that have style issues.

One term I capitalize, although the recent *Chicago Manual of Style* makes it a lowercase term, is *Civil Rights Movement*. In the *Chicago Manual of Style*, 14th edition, the term *Civil Rights Movement* appears with initial caps. In the 15th edition of the stylebook, this term is lowercased. I capitalize it because I reason that the Civil Rights Movement is ongoing and continues in the 21st century and therefore should be initial caps. When I use that term in a document, I always put the capitalized term on my Style Sheet. The Style Sheet accompanies my work when I send it to an editor. But I am aware that I am taking exception to the rule.

In reading this book, have you noticed what words in the text I have capitalized and what words I have left lowercased? I capitalize the terms *Digital Age* and *Style Sheet*. I lowercase the terms *web* and *website*.

Contractions

In the 21st century, even whether you use contractions in your writing is considered part of the mechanical style. A debate continues among language people as to whether using all contractions in a piece makes it too informal and using no contractions makes a piece too formal. This is a primary example of how mechanical detail contributes to style.

Rosa Parks *wouldn't* give up her seat on the bus. She remained resolute and the bus driver *couldn't* make her move.
Rosa Parks *would not* give up her seat on the bus. She remained resolute and the bus driver *could not* make her move.

If you are a student, check with your advisor or professors as to the school's preference. When writing a job-related report, ask your employer whether the company has a preference regarding contractions. Contractions are not used, for example, in most textbooks for primary and secondary schools. And people I polled who work in the legal field say they never use contractions in their legal writing.

Be aware that contractions are an issue. Whatever you decide—whether to use or not use contractions—note that on your Style Sheet that you keep for each document you write.

Grammar

Verbs

The mechanics of the sentences you create include grammar and how you use specific parts of speech. How you use verbs has a strong impact on your style. Whether you use the active or passive voice is part of the form of your writing and is part of the way you relate content. Always using the passive voice in a document sets a slower pace to your writing. Writing moves along at a faster pace if you use the active voice with specific verbs. This is where mechanics—the specific voice of verbs—contribute to the clarity and tone of your writing style.

Look at your writing. Do you use precise verbs, or do you rely on variations of the verb *to be*? The various forms of the verb *to be* are the most overused verb in English writing. We are all guilty of this characteristic of writing in English.

Vague: Joe is coming to visit us this summer.
Specific: Joe plans to visit us this July.

Verbals

Forms of verbs that work in sentences as different parts of speech are called *verbals*. We discussed verbals in the grammar chapter (chapter 2), and you might want to reread that section. Basically, gerunds are verbs that act as nouns and end with an *ing* or *ed* ending. Participles are verbs that also end in *ing* or *ed*, but they work in sentences as adjectives or adverbs. Infinitives are verbals that do the job of a noun, an adjective, or an adverb.

Routinely check your writing for the overuse of verbals. If you use many verbals, you reduce the power of verbs in your writing. Consider these two sentences that use noun forms of verbs instead of action verbs. I think they are rather convoluted sentences.

> Despite President Ellsworth's knowledge that the college had *a need* for new grants for the *improvement* of its research laboratory, she expressed *hesitation* in making *applications* for grants. She wanted to give *encouragement* for *an increase* of donations by the college alumni.

Now consider a rewrite—one sentence that uses action verbs instead of the noun forms of the verbs.

> Though President Ellsworth *knew* the college *needed* new grants *to improve* its laboratory, she *hesitated to apply* for grants because she wanted *to encourage* the college alumni *to increase* their donations.

The six actions in the rewrite are all represented by the same part of speech—they are all verbs. And that part of speech—the verb—is why we think this rewrite is clearer.

Numbers

How you style numbers throughout a written piece is part of the mechanics of style. Do you write out all numbers in words? Do you write some numbers in digits? When you cite a decade, do you use an apostrophe before the *s*, such as *1960's*, or do you delete it? Do you delete the century and just write *60s*? Or perhaps you write out the word as *sixties*, or do you cap it? All these details are part of the number style of your piece. Note the various ways the decade of the 1960s can be rendered:

1960s	1960's
60s	60's
sixties	Sixties

A common style used by writers and editors is to spell out numbers one through nine and use digits for 10 upward. Approximate numbers are usually spelled out. Digits are always used for percentages: 15 percent, 33 percent.

The recent *Chicago* manual calls for spelling out numbers from zero through 100 and using digits only after 100. *Chicago* does cite, as an alternative style, the spelling of numbers one through nine and using digits for 10 upward. Check *Chicago* for the styling of different categories of numbers, such as money and large numbers. Numbers beginning a sentence are always spelled out.

Do you notice number styles in your reading? The *New Yorker Magazine*, for example, writes out most numbers used in articles. Newspapers online usually use digits to save space. Whatever number style you select, record it on your Style Sheet for the document and use the same number style consistently throughout the piece.

Punctuation

Mechanics also include punctuation. Do you use open punctuation? Are your sentences complex? Are you sure the reader will understand your sentences in the open punctuation style? Do you use close punctuation—that is, use as many commas as you can legally use? If so, remember that close punctuation slows down the reader. Is that your intent? Do you use dashes instead of semicolons? Remember that all internal punctuation determines the pace at which a reader reads your sentences. Internal punctuation helps create a rhythm to sentences.

> *Open punctuation*: This past summer Laura and Calvin drove an electric car to San Francisco and then they drove to Vancouver.
> *Close punctuation*: This past summer, Laura and Calvin drove an electric car to San Francisco, and then they drove to Vancouver.

Be sure to record on your document Style Sheet the punctuation style you select to use—then use it consistently!

Back-to-Back Vowels

You can find a discussion about back-to-back vowels when using prefixes and hyphens in the punctuation chapter under hyphens (see chapter 1). The common usage was to use hyphens when a prefix ends in a vowel such as *anti* and the root word begins with a vowel such as *establishment—anti-establishment*. It was called hyphenating back-to-back vowels. Another example is *anti-organization*.

In the 21st century, however, this rule no longer applies. Merriam-Webster Online and its print version close up the words *antiestablishment* and *antiorganization*. The *American Heritage Dictionary* also closes up these words.

Be aware that this question of whether to hyphenate back-to-back vowels is an ongoing issue. As a student writing papers for school, you should check with your advisor or professors to learn what the school preference is. If you are writing a report for work, be sure to ask your employer what the company style is. Most companies have a company Style Sheet that addresses this issue.

Citing Resources Used for Facts

How you cite the resources you use in gathering facts for your document is considered part of the mechanics of style. What stylebook you select to use determines the mechanics of your footnotes, endnotes, and bibliography. Some stylebooks call for extensive information in endnotes and footnotes. Others prefer the shortened form of citations. As discussed in chapter 3, if you are a student, check with your professors or advisors about what stylebook the school suggests. This is especially important to do if you are a graduate student working in a specialized area of expertise. Many specialized fields have specific stylebooks for styling endnotes, footnotes, and bibliographies.

Be sure to list on your Style Sheet the title and edition of the stylebook you use for your citations. Be consistent in following the style of the various types of endnotes, footnotes, and bibliography of a document.

Final word: Whatever mechanics you decide to use, record them on a Style Sheet, and use them consistently throughout the document you are writing.

Substance

The two essential parts of the substance of your document are the content itself—the facts and information you include—and the manner in which you present that content. The content of a written piece works with the mechanics (form) to create style. It is the relationship between form and content that creates a style.

To use relevant content and to express the content in a clear manner with a logical flow, ask yourself the following questions about the document you are writing.

What is the overall objective of the document? Is it written, for example, to inform, to educate, to advocate, to entertain, to inspire, or to debate?

Is the document aimed at a specific audience? All sorts of niche audiences exist in the 21st century. You might be writing a document aimed at academics, politicians, residents of a specific geographic area (such as urban or suburban), or a group of experts such as techies, bankers, historians, medical workers, or investment brokers. Your document might be aimed at a particular age group.

Once you decide your reason for writing the piece and the audience you are targeting, begin by organizing your content. Writing an outline that includes the facts and information you will use helps structure the flow of the piece. In writing your outline, ask yourself: What will be the focus of your piece? And what will be the unifying elements to the piece?

In organizing the information, consider how you will start the piece—will you immediately state the issue and then recap the background of that issue? Or will you start with a chronology and lead up to the current issue? In your organizing outline, include adequate transitions from idea to idea so the facts and points you make are integrated. And make sure there is a cohesive conclusion.

I stress the importance of developing an outline. Once you plan the structure of the piece, you can focus on the language and writing good sentences and paragraphs.

Words and Sentences

The basic formula for writing is: words create sentences; sentences create paragraphs; and paragraphs create an essay or story or book. Writing starts with words. Sentences, as stated in the grammar chapter (chapter 2), are made up of verbs, nouns, pronouns, adjectives, adverbs, conjunctions, prepositions, and interjections—all these types of words have specific jobs they do in sentences.

Look carefully at the words you use. Your word choices determine your clarity—your essential writing style. Do you use clear, specific words and phrases in sentences that demonstrate a grasp of the subject? Or are your word choices vague and pretentious and convey some confusion?

> *Pretentious, vague description*: Jennifer's first job was working as a *relationship manager* at Macy's.
>> This sentence is both pretentious and vague. What is a *relationship manager*?
> *Clear description*: Jennifer's first job was as a salesperson at Macy's.
>> Working as a salesperson at Macy's was Jennifer's first job.

Specificity

It is important to be specific in your writing. I repeat this advice and discuss it further in chapter 5. Use precise words, especially verbs and nouns, and avoid vague language in any sentence. Let's consider this sentence:

> Juan went to the store.

This sentence is *correct*. It has a subject, *Juan*; a verb, *went*; and an object, *store*. The sentence has all the *right* elements. But if this sentence were the first sentence in a short story recommended to me by a friend, I would not read any further than this first sentence. I would also question my friend's recommendation.

Why would I not read further? This sentence is a classic example of a vague, boring sentence. This sentence lacks specificity and tells me next to nothing. Everything in this sentence is general. But let's rescue this sentence and make some changes.

> We add a specific verb: Juan ran to the store.
> We change the object to a specific type of store: Juan ran to the drugstore.
> We add an adjective to the specific type of store: Juan ran to the all-night drugstore.
> We add an adverb phrase to specifically tell when Juan ran to the all-night drugstore: Juan ran to the all-night drugstore at 3 a.m.

We could make other more drastic changes by adding more specific information. Remember that every sentence can be written at least five different ways—here are three suggestions. Can you think of two other ways this sentence could be written?

> At 3 a.m. Juan ran to the 24-hour drugstore to pick up a prescription for his ailing grandmother.
> Juan dashed to the all-night drugstore at 3 a.m. to refill his ailing grandmother's prescription.
> At 3 a.m. Juan bolted to the 24-hour drugstore to refill his ailing grandmother's prescription.

It is not necessary to use five-dollar words to be specific. But you do have to use precise words correctly in your sentences and avoid useless, wordy phrases. Various lists of wordy phrases are on the web and in language books. Below is a sampling of such phrases that do not add any meaning to sentences and take up space:

the fact that	in my opinion	my view is
in the event of	with a view to	direct your attention to
it is likely that	in the final analysis	at such time
is focused on	in some instances	to which I replied

Slant and Spin

Just about everything written, including e-mails, has a slant or spin. In the 20th century, discussions about writing mentioned the *slant* of a written piece. In the 21st century, we are more likely to discuss the *spin* of a written piece.

Content—the facts you include in your document—and the words used can create a spin to your writing. Unless you are assigned to write an advocacy piece, check your work for slant/spin issues. Even in writing an advocacy piece, remember that there is a difference between writing a slant/spin into a written piece and writing a persuasive argument. Slant/spin usually highlights only a few selected facts, and only one side of the issue is presented. Extreme language and exaggerated facts are usually two excesses of slant/spin in writing.

Review your writing for slant/spin and ask yourself three questions: Did I cite relevant, truthful facts, or are they questionable or exaggerated? Are my conclusions reasonable, or are they extreme? What is the overall tone of the written piece?

One Last Word

To recognize characteristics of style in your writing, read, read, read. Many of my students, when I ask them what they read, reply that they "read everything." That's a good habit, but I encourage you to read and *critically assess* everything you read. That is an even better habit.

To easily assess style when you read, practice reviewing what mechanics the writer used in the document you are reading and how language is used. What verbs are used? Are specific nouns used or does the writer use many adjectives?

Look also at the overall organization of the content. Does the author start off with a main idea expressed in the first paragraph? Does the author expand on the main idea in subsequent paragraphs?

Become very familiar with the mechanics and language issues discussed in this chapter and throughout this book. Remember that any writer can write each sentence in a document at least five different ways. The humanist and Greek professor Erasmus believed each sentence could be written 150 ways! In your spare time, you might try writing a sentence 150 different ways. But you get the point—words are flexible.

Decide the method you prefer of reviewing your work—printing out the document and reviewing on paper with pencil, or reviewing your work online. Many people prefer reviewing their work on paper and claim they *see more* on paper than reviewing online. Below are some essential questions you should ask yourself about your written document.

Overall Organization
1. What is the purpose of the document you are writing? Who is the audience?

2. How does the document begin and end? Is the last paragraph redundant, or does it leave the reader with fresh ideas to think about?

Mechanics

3. Do you use verbs in the active or passive voice?

4. How often do you use a form of the verb *to be*? Instead, use specific verbs.

5. Do the subject and verb agree in number in your sentences?

6. How many gerunds and participles do you use?

7. How many prepositional phrases do you use? Can they be deleted or replaced with verbs or other specific wording?

8. What voice do you use—the first person "I," the second person "you," or the third person "we"?

Words

9. What words do you select to use? Do you use clear, precise words or obscure words?

10. Do you use formal, pretentious words you looked up in the thesaurus? Or do you use the language you usually speak?

11. Are colloquial expressions or nonstandard American English in your document—and, if so, for what purpose?

12. Did you isolate clichés and wordy phrases and eliminate them?

13. When you read your document aloud, what words clang on your ears?

Overall Flow of Content

14. What punctuation style do you use for word flow? Or do you use a jumbled mix of both the open punctuation and close punctuation styles?

15. Does the content flow in each paragraph from the first sentence in the paragraph?

16. Do you exaggerate in your writing?

17. Do you properly credit quotes you use? Are the quotes used in your document credited with vague references? The vaguest reference, but one very popular in the 21st century, is the "unknown government official who requested ano-nymity."

Finally:

18. In reviewing the piece you wrote, do you feel the document reads well?

Practice

Below is a paragraph of information gathered from a NASA web page about the sun. The author used close punctuation. On each line, identify at least one problem of mechanics or content/substance. Write your answers with their corresponding sentence numbers on a separate sheet of paper.

A. The sun is a star. A star does not have a solid surface, but is a ball of gas. It is held together by

B. it's own gravity. The center of our solar system, the sun makes up 99.8 percent of the mass of

C. the entire solar system. If the sun was as tall as a typical front door, Earth would be a nickel.

D. Since the sun is not a solid body, different parts of the sun rotated at different rates. At the

E. equator, the sun spins once about every 25 days, but at its poles the sun rotates once on its axis

F. every thirty-six Earth days. The solar atmosphere, which is a thin layer of gases, is where we

G. see features such as sunspots and solar flares on the sun. Spacecraft are constantly increasingly

H. our understanding of the sun. The space craft Genesis collected samples of the solar wind and

I. returned the particles to Earth. The sun is orbited by 12 plants, tens of thousands of asteroids,

J. and approximate three trillion comets and icy bodies.

Notes

1. Norman Borlaug obituary, Associated Press, accessed August 13, 2013, https://groups.google.com/forum/#!topic/alt.obituaries/zqrC7R0LoCY.

2. Norman Borlaug obituary, *New York Times*, accessed August 13, 2013, http://www.nytimes.com/2009/09/14/business/energy-environment/14borlaug.html?pagewanted=all&_r=.

3. Aristotle, *Rhetoric and the Poetics*, trans. W. Rhys Roberts and Ingram Bywater (New York: Random House, 1984), 167, 168.

4. William Strunk Jr. and E. B. White, *The Elements of Style*, 4th ed. (New York: Longman, 1979), 70–81.

5. Aristotle, *Rhetoric*, 174, 175.

CHAPTER FIVE
VOICE—EVERY WRITER'S GOAL

Voice is the intangible that makes writing memorable. Just like the sound of your spoken voice, your written voice can have a *sound* to it. By that, I mean your written voice can have characteristics usually attributed to sound—such as soft, shrill, hesitant, arrogant, or loud.

Voice is the most elusive aspect to create in your writing. Much of what we read daily really doesn't have a voice—the sentences and paragraphs are not read and reread and are not particularly memorable. But writing that has a voice is memorable and read throughout centuries.

Explaining voice in writing is a bit like discussing alchemy—and humans have debated both subjects for eons. The word *voice* in regard to writing is often used interchangeably with *style*. I consider style a different element from voice. Style, as discussed in chapter 4, is the mechanics and substance of a written piece. Writing can have style, giving it clarity and coherence, but not be memorable—not have a voice. But for a written piece to have a voice, it must also have a style. Should I move on to alchemy now?

Writers, critics, and even philosophers have tried to analyze for centuries what makes writing have a voice. I recommend you start thinking about voice in your writing and read a few of those discussions, both classical and contemporary. And especially read what well-known writers of all centuries say about style and voice.

In *The Elements of Style*, E. B. White says that there is no way to analyze what makes some writing memorable and other writing pedestrian. He calls his famous Chapter V, in which he discusses writing that he describes as "distinguished and distinguishing," a "mystery story, thinly disguised." I agree that what makes some writing seem to sing off the page and other writing clang on the page is a bit of a mystery. It is useful for writers, however, to explore and aim to have a voice in their writing. It is also especially important that writers be able to identify a voice in writing. I offer below a basic discussion of the interplay of writing essentials and the elusive aspect of voice.

Voice

Voice in a written piece happens when various essentials work together in a kind of harmony. Those elements include form or the punctuation, grammar, and mechanics of a piece.

Punctuation and grammar can convey feelings and attitude, elements that are part of a written voice. The dash, particularly in fiction, can convey a sharp interruption suggesting abruptness or annoyance. A character in a story who speaks hesitantly can be portrayed by always having the character's words end in ellipses. Remember that in the punctuation and grammar chapters (chapters 1 and 2), I stressed that both of these essentials should enhance the flow of your writing—not clog it. Are these essentials intrusive, or do they help create a smooth flow of language in your writing?

Content, or the substance of a piece, is another necessary element to examine when looking at voice. This is particularly important in nonfiction writing. Does the piece have substance—have solid facts or something significant to say or report or advocate? Does the document have credibility?

Your writing also has to subtly express your feelings and values to have a voice. This is different from letting your personality dominate the writing. *Subtly* is the key word here. This characteristic of voice is the most delicate to execute well, and it is truly a large part of the art of memorable writing. Even if you are writing an opinion column or advocacy blog, do not overstate or hammer your opinions, feelings, or values into your writing. Instead, create writing that artfully expresses your opinions, feelings, and values.

What joins these essentials into a voice? Words. The words you choose to use and the manner in which you present those words reveal something of yourself—your voice. And when that happens in writing, you create something far greater than alchemy—memorable writing.

Words, Words, Words

Essentials

1. The words you select should subtly reveal something about your values and feelings.

2. The words you select and how you use them greatly contribute to how memorable your writing is.

3. You should know how to use the denotation and connotation of words.

4. A facility with words is essential to creating voice in your writing.

It is crucial you understand that the words you select and how you use those words in your writing reveal something about you. It is how you put *yourself* into your writing. Let that fact seep into your soul—or your conscious and subconscious, if you prefer. Do you use formal, informal, or even colloquial words in your writing? Do you use words you looked up in the thesaurus and never use in your daily speech? Do your sentences have many adverbs because you use vague verbs? In chapter 4, which discusses style, I talked about using specific words for clarity. In this chapter, I discuss using specific words to put yourself into your writing and create a voice.

All the analogies used to describe words are appropriate here: words are to writing as paints are to painting; words are as important to writing as musical notes are to music. I particularly like the comparison to music. Words basically create the sentences and paragraphs and create the *tone*—the *sound*—of a written piece. As musical notes reveal the values and feelings of a composer, word selection can reveal the values and feelings of you, the author.

Specific words in sentences and paragraphs that you write, like notes in a symphony, can convey your feelings of joy, sadness, fear, hope, despair, even nationalism and freedom—any of your feelings, values, and attitudes. This we call voice—the sound you, the author, writes that *lifts* off the page. And voice in a written piece makes the piece memorable.

Specific Words

Again I urge you to use specific words. Avoid using too many adjectives and adverbs. Use a specific noun or verb rather than describing general nouns and verbs with adjectives and adverbs. If you must describe nouns and verbs, be specific in your use of adjectives and adverbs.

Consider the words used in describing a place where people live— *house, home, cabin, hut, bungalow, split-level, ranch, mansion, dwelling, castle,* or even *shelter.* These nouns are synonyms for a place where people live. None of these synonyms have exactly the same meaning. Each conjures up a different image. Instead of using the word *house* with an adjective, select a specific word to describe the place where your characters live.

As discussed earlier, specific words help compose the sound of your writing. In music, the sound is called the *timbre* and refers to the quality of tone. Timbre is often called the *tone color* of music. It is like the color in painting. Words used to describe the tone color of music include *harsh, warm, mellow, shrill, choppy, piercing, strident, heavy, dark, bright, joyful,* or even *eerie.* Those same words are often used to describe the qualities of tone in writing. A good way to identify timbre in a sentence is to read it aloud.

Is the tone color of this opening sentence of an essay on the federal government's student loan policy positive or negative and rather harsh? Look at the specific words used.

> The federal government once again has skewered the student loan application process so that it requires hiring a "loan consultant" to accurately complete the mass of paperwork necessary to receive a loan.

The word *skewered* and the phrase *mass of paperwork* express a somewhat harsh negativity in describing the student loan program. Can you think of other ways to describe the student loan program that are perhaps less negative and harsh? Practice rewriting this sentence, and in your rewrite express a different tone.

Historic Advice

As discussed in chapter 4, Aristotle has some worthy advice about using specific words in writing. He discusses nouns, verbs, and prepositions in *Rhetoric*. In *Poetics* he really addresses word selection. He analyzes what he calls *lexis*—language—the choice of written words that are clear and effective. Scholar Stephen Halliwell points out in his book, *Aristotle's Poetics*, that this section on language is the second longest section of *Poetics* after the analysis of plot and structure. Aristotle considered word choice an essential part of writing well.

Aristotle uses the term *diction*, which means the choice of words used for clearness and effectiveness—whether for text or speech. Stephen Halliwell translates his comments about diction as "Excellence of diction means clarity and avoidance of banality."[1]

Aristotle says that "clearest is the diction that uses standard terms, but this is banal. . . . Impressive and above the ordinary is the diction that uses exotic language (by 'exotic' I mean loan words, metaphors, lengthenings and all divergence from the standard)."[2] He talks of a harmony or blend: "One needs then a certain blend of these components . . . [that] will create an impression that is neither ordinary nor banal, while standard terms will ensure clarity."[3]

Stephen Halliwell interprets Aristotle's advice to writers as "be clear without being commonplace."[4] That's good advice to writers in any century—be clear, but be unique. How do you do that? You gain a facility with words by routinely exercising your writing skills. As most composers immerse themselves in music, writers should immerse themselves in words and habitually practice writing. Take sentences or paragraphs from a newspaper, magazine, or blog on the Internet, and write the sentences or paragraphs at least five different ways. Look at your rewrites. Did you use vague verbs and unspecified nouns in the rewrites? Did you use many nonessential clauses? Were your rewrites longer or shorter than the originals? Prose that is clear and unique uses words to create specificity of people, places, and action.

Degrees, Values, and Attitude

On the most elementary level, all parts of speech in American English have words that express degree (or intensity or levels), value, and attitude.

Verbs, for example, can describe specific degrees or intensity of action. The verbs in these sentences below all convey a specific degree of work that Ellen did on her dissertation.

> Ellen edited her dissertation.
>> This sentence above vaguely describes the work Ellen did. The sentences below describe more specifically the work Ellen did.
> Ellen rewrote her dissertation.
> Ellen polished her dissertation.

Similarly, use specific words to convey your attitude and values. The sentence below states a fact—plain and simple. There is no attitude or value given in this sentence:

> Shirley wore a green hat with a tassel all last winter.

Consider adding value words:

> Shirley wore a green hat with a silly tassel all during last year's severe winter.

The sentence above has some of the author's values. It tells me the author does not value the tassel on Shirley's hat. It is not a neutral sentence. There is some tone to the sentence.

Consider adding attitude words to this sentence that conveys a fact.

> Alec decided to exercise every day.

Give Alec an attitude:

> Alec firmly decided to exercise every day.
> Alex enthusiastically decided to exercise every day.

Tone

To gain an ease with choosing words that create *tone* in writing, read prose and poetry. I recommend especially reading poetry—all sorts of poetry, including classical, Renaissance, modern, and 21st-century poetry. In poetry it is easy to see how the specific choice of words determines the sensibility and tone color of the poem and whether the sound of the poem lifts off the page. Explore Internet sites for poetry of all ages. Both poems presented here are on the Project Gutenberg website.

For poems that soar off pages, read the poetry of Gerard Manley Hopkins. He was born in 1844 in England and, while attending Oxford, converted to Catholicism. He became a Jesuit and eventually taught Greek at the Royal University in Dublin. Though he lived in the Victorian Age, his poems defied the typical Victorian poetry. However, none of his poems were ever published in his lifetime. Consider his poem "Pied-Beauty." Note the unusual words—what Aristotle would call "all divergent from the standard." Certainly the words Hopkins uses are not banal. This poem sings if you read it silently; if you read it aloud, you might think you are reciting an aria.

> Glory be to God for dappled things—
> For skies of couple-colour as a brinded cow;
> For rose-moles all in stipple upon trout that swim;
> Fresh-firecoal chestnut-falls; finches' wings;
> Landscape plotted and pieced—fold, fallow, and plough;
> And áll trádes, their gear and tackle and trim.
>
> All things counter, original, spare, strange;
> Whatever is fickle, freckled (who knows how?)
> With swift, slow; sweet, sour; adazzle, dim;
> He fathers-forth whose beauty is past change:
> Praise him.

Another poem I suggest you read for language is "Ode to a Nightingale" by John Keats. The words are not quite as unusual as in the Hopkins poem, but the flow of the language and the thoughts expressed are memorable.

> Thou wast not born for death, immortal Bird!
> No hungry generations tread thee down;
> The voice I hear this passing night was heard
> In ancient days by emperor and clown:

> Perhaps the self-same song that found a path
> Through the sad heart of Ruth, when, sick for home,
> She stood in tears amid the alien corn;
> The same that oft-times hath
> Charmed magic casements, opening on the foam
> Of perilous seas, in faery lands forlorn.

The language flows in melody, and what Keats says about the nightingale's song and the emperor and the clown is sheer wisdom. Remember that in the Digital Age, American English is changing—but take solace. The nightingale's song and all birdsong haven't and undoubtedly will not change in the Digital Age!

Denotation and Connotation

Understand that the *definition* of each word helps create the *tone* in writing. To recap: Merriam-Webster defines *tone* as "a quality, feeling, or attitude expressed by the words that someone uses in speaking or writing." In using American English, we are fortunate. Most of our words have two types of definitions. These are called the *denotation* and the *connotation*.

Denotation is the literal definition of the word. Connotation is the implied meaning and the feelings the word evokes—the emotional reaction that the words cause in the reader.

In this chapter we have talked about the different words that describe a place where people live. The word *home* was one of those words. Merriam-Webster defines *home* as literally the place where a person lives. In this sentence, the denotation of the word is used:

Natalie and Frank live in a *home* on Lakeview Road.

This is a sentence that states a fact; it does not convey a feeling or attitude. Usually in the context in which the denotation of a word is used, nothing is suggested or implied and no feeling, value, or attitude is expressed.

The connotation of the word *home*, however, means much more. The word *home* has an implied or emotional association; it can convey feeling or attitude.

> Though Ravi has lived in the United States for five years, he still considers India his *home*.

Here the word *home* means more than the place where a person lives. The sentence conveys that Ravi no longer physically lives in India—he lives in the United States—but he has an emotional attachment, a feeling, and an attitude about India. The sentence conveys much more than the literal meaning of the word *home*. By using the connotative meaning of the word *home*, the author has expressed Ravi's feeling and attitude; the sentence has *tone*.

Connotations help shape reader's responses. Connotations are powerful word tools.

Remember that you can write each sentence at least five different ways, and that includes this sentence about Ravi and his feelings about India. Are these sentences better or worse?

1. For five years Ravi has lived in the United States, but he is still attached to India.

2. Ravi arrived in the United States five years ago, yet he still has fond feelings about his native India.

3. Ravi has lived for five years in the United States but still has a deep attachment to India.

4. Although Ravi lives in the United States, he talks affectionately about his native India.

5. Ravi lives in the United States, but he still calls India his home.

As you can see, sentences 1–4 just explain Ravi's feelings and are rather *flat*—or lacking in an expressive tone. And one sentence is in the passive voice. Those sentences also use many words as compared to sentence 5, which is succinctly written and uses *home* in a connotative manner.

Pay attention to the denotation and connotation of American English words. Many words in our culture can imply or suggest and evoke feelings and emotion. I repeat that connotative meanings of words are powerful word tools. Learn to use them.

Synonyms

Every discussion of voice must include a mention of synonyms. They give a sentence different tone color or shading or gradations. Having a good command of synonyms can help you add value and attitude to your writing.

Synonyms can have similar meanings, but not the exact same meaning. Be very specific in the synonyms you choose to use. What, for example, are the subtle differences in *Laura yelled*, *Laura shouted*, and *Laura screamed*? If you use a thesaurus, be sure to look up the meaning of any word you are considering using. Read all the word's dictionary meanings, and pay attention to the word's etymology. Merriam-Webster Online dictionary includes a list of synonyms with each word's definition. Become familiar with that feature.

Consider the subtle differences and gradations that these synonyms evoke:

happy	gathering
content	assemblage
cheerful	meeting
equal	school
interchangeable	academy
parallel	seminary
work	tired
function	droopy-eyed
occupation	exhausted

A Written Voice

Now let's examine the tone color of an opening to an acclaimed book. Does this opening have voice—the values, attitudes, and feelings of the writer?

The book is *The History of the Standard Oil Company* by Ida M. Tarbell. It sounds like a boring book, but it is anything but that. Ida Tarbell's compelling history of the oil trust built by John D. Rockefeller has lasted over a century.

The text of the book was first published in a series of articles in *Mc-Clure's* magazine in 1903. *McClure's* was a popular publication in the United States in the early 20th century. Tarbell's writing about the Standard Oil Company captivated the nation and eventually led to the dissolution of the Standard Oil Trust—the business structure that monopolized the oil industry. In 1911, the Supreme Court ordered the Standard Oil Trust be broken up into smaller companies.

Though you might not like history, look at Tarbell's skillful and artful exposé of John D. Rockefeller's Standard Oil Trust. Ida Tarbell was considered a muckraker, better known in the 21st century as an investigative journalist. In 1999, Tarbell's exposé was selected fifth of the top one hundred works of 20th-century journalism in America. Tarbell has been called one of the "most accomplished non-fiction writers of her time."[5]

Let's closely examine the opening paragraph of her work that tells the story of the Standard Oil Trust. To begin, read the paragraph in its entirety.

One of the busiest corners of the globe at the opening of the year 1872 was a strip of Northwestern Pennsylvania, not over fifty miles long, known the world over as the Oil Regions. Twelve years before this strip of land had been but little better than a wilderness; its chief inhabitants the lumbermen, who every season cut great swaths of primeval pine and hemlock from its hills, and in the spring floated them down the Allegheny River to Pittsburg. The great tides of Western emigration had shunned the spot for years as too rugged and unfriendly for settlement, and yet in twelve years this region avoided by men had been transformed into a bustling trade centre, where towns elbowed each other for place, into which three great trunk railroads had built branches, and every foot of whose soil was fought for by capitalists. It was the discovery and development of a new raw product, petroleum, which had made this change from wilderness to market-place. This product in twelve years had not only peopled a waste place of the earth, it had revolutionised [*sic*] the world's methods of illumination and added millions upon millions of dollars to the wealth of the United States.[6]

The opening paragraph is just five sentences. But Ida Tarbell's opening is energetic and draws the reader into a world of change wrought by oil.

Tarbell opens the book by describing the changes that oil effected and then goes on to describe oil—the cause of this change. This reversal of cause and effect in narrative to effect and cause in this narrative puts the focus on change. She does not open the book in the usual cause-and-effect structure by commonly stating: In 1871, oil was discovered in Northwestern Pennsylvania and the area grew—blah, blah, blah. She grips the reader in the opening paragraph by first portraying the change—the momentum—that oil has generated.

First sentence: *One of the busiest corners of the globe at the opening of the year 1872 was a strip of Northwestern Pennsylvania, not over fifty miles long, known the world over as the Oil Regions.*

This opening sentence establishes place (Northwestern Pennsylvania), and she does that by encompassing the world—*one of the busiest corners of the globe* and *known the world over*. She doesn't just establish the setting in the United States for her story—her story is important to the world. She then juxtaposes the world with a *strip of Northwestern Pennsylvania, not over fifty miles long*. She is telling us that just a *strip* of land has world importance. The word *strip* gives the sentence tone—subtly tells us her view: to her, a little bit of land is having a great impact in the world. She doesn't convey that fact in a dry, factual sentence. By using words and phrases like *busiest corner of the globe*, *the world over*, and *strip of land*, she ties the universal (globe, world) to the particular—a strip of land in Pennsylvania. She composes a sentence that captures the reader and draws the reader into her narrative of change—oil, the Oil Regions, and the world.

Second sentence: *Twelve years before this strip of land had been but little better than a wilderness; its chief inhabitants the lumbermen, who every season cut great swaths of primeval pine and hemlock from its hills, and in the spring floated them down the Allegheny River to Pittsburg.*

Here Tarbell gives background to the area. She does this splendidly in her imagery—*wilderness* (not rural area), *lumbermen*, and *great swaths of primeval pine*. You get the atmosphere of ruggedness. Read this sentence aloud—it has a great vocal sound to it.

Third sentence: *The great tides of Western emigration had shunned the spot for years as too rugged and unfriendly for settlement, and yet in twelve years this region avoided by men had been transformed into a bustling trade centre, where towns elbowed each other for place, into which three great trunk railroads had built branches, and every foot of whose soil was fought for by capitalists.*

This is the longest sentence in the paragraph, and perhaps too long. But consider the language—*emigration had shunned the spot*—not "immigrants had avoided the area," but rather a whole movement, emigration. And her choice of the word *shunned*—this is one of those words with an intensity—a slightly different meaning than if she used the commonplace word *avoided.* Perhaps now in the 21st century, the phrase *bustling trade center* seems like a trite expression and needs work. But the phrase *where towns elbowed each other for place* is a great uncommon use of the verb *elbowed.* She adds some drama in the phrase *every foot of whose soil was fought for by capitalists.* By referring to *every foot*, she avoids using such a pedestrian phrase such as "capitalists fought for the land."

Fourth sentence: *It was the discovery and development of a new raw product, petroleum, which had made this change from wilderness to market-place.*

This is a short sentence after a long one, and such variance adds rhythm. She describes oil as *a new raw product.* This use of the word *raw* makes this description stand out. The product is not only new but also in a natural state. I think this ties in to some degree with the description of the wilderness in sentence 2. Everything about oil—the product and the place where it is found—has a wildness, an untamed characteristic about it. So far she has implied that everything is new in this old wilderness, and it is so important that it is known to the world.

Fifth sentence: *This product in twelve years had not only peopled a waste place of the earth, it had revolutionised [sic] the world's methods of illumination and added millions upon millions of dollars to the wealth of the United States.*

After establishing change, place, and the wonder of the discovery of petroleum, she now relates the importance of petroleum. In this sentence, she begins to establish the significance of petroleum and what it had done.

After reading Tarbell's opening, ask yourself how you write about a subject that causes change. Do you first capture the momentum surrounding the subject? Does that unique opening make you want to keep reading this story of the Standard Oil Trust? Ida Tarbell's narrative is considered a classic and continues to be popular today. Remember, writing that has a voice is read for centuries.

One Last Word

Developing a writing voice and gaining ease with making artful word choices takes practice. Read, read, read, and write, write, write. Most good writers, when talking about the writing process, usually talk of choosing words almost by instinct. At some point, *you* will gain an instinct in word choice.

To feed this word instinct, continue to read and write and apply your critical assessment skills to what you read and write. Assess how the essentials that we reviewed in earlier chapters work together in what you read and write.

And, most importantly, gain a facility with words—collect words, sign up for a free Word a Day e-mail, browse the dictionary, and even keep your own personal dictionary. What type of words do you use in your writing? What is your written voice?

Always give your writing a final check for the items discussed in this chapter. Below are some essential questions you should ask yourself about your voice in a written document. Ask yourself, first, if it is appropriate for you to include your attitude and values in the document you are writing: Is it a job-related factual report type of assignment? A news report that requires neutral information? Such assignments would require restraining your attitude, values, and feelings in the document.

1. Do you express yourself subtly in your document or do you use heavy-handed words to express your attitudes and values?

2. Do you only use the denotative meanings of words or do you at least occasionally use the connotative meaning of words?

3. Again, do you use different verbs from the verb forms of *to be*?

4. Do you use too many adjectives and adverbs? Look to use specific nouns and verbs.

5. Overall, do you select words that are clear and unique?

6. Have you read your essay aloud? If so, is there a tone to your document?

7. And finally, do you think all the essentials in your written piece work in harmony?

Practice

A student recently reread *David Copperfield* by Charles Dickens and wrote this brief description. On a separate sheet of paper, list each word that appears in italics. In the context of the paragraph, identify whether each word is used in its denotative or connotative meaning. If the writer used the connotative meaning of a word, explain what is implied; if a word is used in its denotative meaning, include that specific meaning.

A. Having just reread the *classic* novel *David Copperfield*, I found to my surprise that

B. I still enjoyed the series of *challenges* Copperfield confronted and resolved. He *built*

C. a *new* life despite being orphaned when only a child. His great aunt

D. took him *under her wing* and arranged for his education and his *settling* on

E. a profession. He *fell in love* with a *slight*, pretty, young woman and married her.

F. Many readers think his wife Dora was *childish*, others think Dora *childlike*. All

G. readers agree, however, that the *snake* in the novel is well-defined. Uriah

H. Heep, even *now*, remains a *vile* and memorable character in literature.

Notes

1. Aristotle, *Poetics*, ed. and trans. Stephen Halliwell, The Loeb Classical Library (Cambridge, MA: Harvard University Press, 1995), 109.

2. Ibid., 109.

3. Ibid., 111.

4. Stephen Halliwell, *Aristotle's Poetics* (Chicago: University of Chicago Press, 1968, 1998), 346.

5. *American Experience*, "A Journalistic Masterpiece," PBS, accessed September 9, 2013, http://www.pbs.org/wgbh/americanexperience/features/primary-resources/rockefellers-mcclures/.

6. Ida M. Tarbell, *The History of the Standard Oil Company* (Gloucester, MA: Peter Smith, 1963), 3.

CHAPTER SIX
ONE FINAL WORD

One more bit of advice for writing well in the 21st century: make a Style Sheet for every document you write. A Style Sheet records the style of the mechanics—the punctuation, number style, grammar, capitalization, vocabulary, and references—in a document. A Style Sheet is a necessary tool to use in maintaining consistency of style in a document. Most organizations, schools, companies, and publishing houses have a unifying Style Sheet documenting their "house" style. The *New York Times* has an entire book explaining the newspaper's style and usage.

Organizations amend Style Sheets as English usage warrants. For example, the name Massachusetts Institute of Technology was once abbreviated as M.I.T.—with periods after each initial. In the 21st century, the institution now refers to itself as MIT. Obviously, the keeper of MIT's Style Sheet decided to update the style to the 21st century, as periods have been dropped in many abbreviations, such as PhD (which is no longer Ph.D.) and MD (no longer M.D.).

Style Sheets

Essentials

1. Make a Style Sheet for every term paper, dissertation, report, essay, or book that you write. Settle on an overall style consistent with that of your school, organization, or company. This is often called *house*

style or *company style*. Integrate that style into your specific document's Style Sheet.

2. Style Sheets record your specific usage of the mechanics we have discussed in the previous chapters. Every Style Sheet should record the following:

> Reference books and websites used
> Punctuation style—designate open or close punctuation
> Number style
> Trademarks—if no trademarks appear in the text, write "No Trademarks"
> Facts—list pertinent facts that are essential to the document
> Vocabulary list—this is an alphabetical list of hyphenated or closed-up words, the capitalization of all proper nouns, and vocabulary unique to the document

Reference Materials

The first listings on your Style Sheet for a document should be the reference materials you used in writing the document. This includes dictionaries, encyclopedias, style books, and websites you might have visited for information. Be sure to cite which edition of the dictionary or style book you used.

For websites listed other than the dictionary, cite the name of the website, the URL, and the date you accessed the website. Because information on a website changes, the date you accessed a particular website is required except when you access an online dictionary. Writers access an online dictionary so frequently that access dates are not required for dictionary listings.

The Style Sheet for this book would include the following sections.

References

> Merriam-Webster Online: http://www.merriam-webster.com/
> *The Chicago Manual of Style*, 16th edition
> American Library Association, "Using Primary Sources on the Web," American Library Association, accessed July 25, 2013, URL: http://www.ala.org/rusa/resources/usingprimary sources

Encyclopedia of Britannica, entry Erasmus. Accessed August 13, 2013, URL: http://kids.britannica.com/comptons/article-9274195/Desiderius-Erasmus

Internet World Stats: Top Ten Languages on the Internet. Accessed January 15, 2013, URL: http://www.internetworldstats.com/stats7.htm

MIT Classics: Rhetoric by Aristotle. Accessed August 13, 2013, URL: http://classics.mit.edu/Aristotle/rhetoric.3.iii.html

Punctuation Style

The second listing on your Style Sheet for a document indicates the system of punctuation that you are using. List either open or close punctuation. Not everyone understands the two systems of punctuation, so you might explain your punctuation system in more detail, as follows:

Punctuation
Close punctuation—using the serial comma and as much internal punctuation as punctuation rules allow

Number Style

Always include how you style numbers on your Style Sheet—even if there are no numbers in the document.

Number Style
Spell out numbers one through nine. Use digits for 10+
21st century; 20th century
Approximate numbers are spelled out.
Large round numbers: 3 million people; 40 billion dollars
Percent: 40 percent; 50 percent

Grammar Style

The third listing on your Style Sheet should be your grammar style. Mention whether you use active or passive voice. Also mention if you use contractions or do not use contractions. I always indicate whether I use 21st-century usage, such as starting sentences with conjunctions or ending sentences with prepositions.

Grammar
Mostly use active voice, although passive voice is sometimes used.
Use standard contractions.
End some sentences with a preposition.
Start some sentences with a conjunction.
Use a plural pronoun when referencing *everyone* or *everybody*.

Facts

For the fact section, list the facts used in the document that *are not commonly known*. This particularly includes any numbers you cite. In the Introduction, I cite English as the top language used on the Internet. I would list that fact on my Style Sheet. In chapter 5, I mention that Erasmus was a humanist and at one time in his life taught Greek at Cambridge. I would list that fact.

Facts
The number one language used on the Internet is English.
Erasmus was a humanist who lived from 1466 to 1536 and at one time in his life was a teacher of Greek at Cambridge University.
The Elements of Style was first published in 1918 as a style guide for students at Cornell University.

Trademarks

Always have a trademark line on your Style Sheet. If there are trademarks in your document, list them. If there are more than 10 trademarks, have a separate page listing only the trademarks. If there are no trademarks in your document, then state, "No trademarks."

Trademarks discussed in chapter 3 include Levi's, KitchenAid, Xerox.

Vocabulary

The final section to a Style Sheet is an alphabetical vocabulary list. Each document you write, edit, or simply read has a specific vocabulary.

You probably haven't noticed that, but it is important to be aware of the words you are using in your writing and the vocabulary of what you read. The vocabulary list on a Style Sheet includes words that have a style to them—capped words, hyphenated or closed-up words, proper nouns, and unusual words.

Two of the words on the Style Sheet for this book are *website* and *Internet*. In chapter 5, I discuss the different spelling styles for these words. Because these words appear spelled differently in various publications, I include my styling of these words in the vocabulary list.

> *Vocabulary*
> anti-establishment—hyphens used for words with back-to-back
>   vowels in the text
> Digital Age
> e-mail
> Internet
> Merriam-Webster Online
> online
> Punctuation Police
> re-elected
> re-iterate
> Style Sheet
> web
> website

The preliminary Style Sheet for this book looked like this:

Author's Style Sheet for Writing Well in the 21st Century: The Essentials by Linda Spencer

References
Merriam-Webster Online edition: http://www.merriam-webster.com/
The Chicago Manual of Style, 16th edition
American Library Association, "Using Primary Sources on the Web," American Library Association, accessed July 25,

2013, URL: http://www.ala.org/rusa/resources/usingprimary sources

Encyclopedia of Britannica, entry Erasmus. Accessed August 13, 2013, URL: http://kids.britannica.com/comptons/article-9274195/Desiderius-Erasmus

Internet World Stats: Top Ten Languages on the Internet. Accessed January 15, 2013, URL: http://www.internetworld stats.com/stats7.htm

MIT Classics: Rhetoric by Aristotle. Accessed August 13, 2013, URL: http://classics.mit.edu/Aristotle/rhetoric.3.iii.html

Punctuation

Close punctuation—using the serial comma and as much internal punctuation as punctuation rules allow

Number Style

Spell out numbers one through nine. Use digits for 10+
21st century; 20th century
Approximate numbers are spelled out.
Large round numbers: 3 million people; 40 billion dollars
Percent: 40 percent; 50 percent

Grammar

Mostly use active voice, although passive voice is sometimes used.
Use standard contractions.
End some sentences with a preposition.
Start some sentences with a conjunction.
Use a plural pronoun when referencing *everyone* and *everybody*.

Facts

The number one language used on the Internet is English.
Erasmus was a humanist who lived from 1466 to 1536 and at one time in his life was a teacher of Greek at Cambridge University.

The Elements of Style was first published in 1918 as a style guide for students at Cornell University.

Trademarks

Trademarks discussed in chapter 3 include Levi's, KitchenAid, Xerox.

Vocabulary

anti-establishment—hyphens used for words with back-to-back vowels in the text
Digital Age
e-mail
Internet
Merriam-Webster Online
online
Punctuation Police
re-elected
re-iterate
Style Sheet
web
website

Adopt the habit of keeping a Style Sheet as you are writing a document. It keeps the style consistent and helps you see your style. You might find before you finish writing your document that you have changed the style. In writing this book, I decided first to cap *Style Sheet*, then decided to lowercase the term; finally, I capped it.

Remember that good writers want to present their ideas in the best possible writing style—and that takes attention to the details of style.

The Final Word

Punctuation, grammar, facts, style, and voice are essential to every piece you write in the 21st century. Check those essentials when you are writing and in your completed drafts. Take note of those essentials in everything you read.

CHAPTER SIX

Keep abreast of the 21st-century changes in American English, for the language adapts, grows, and invents. Remember that its usage is not determined by the rulings of a lofty national language academy; usage is determined democratically by how people write and speak the language every day. American English embodies democracy. Treasure American English, and use it well.

APPENDIX
Answers to Practices

Chapter 1: Punctuation—The Choices

A. No comma needed after *Before*
B. Correct
C. Correct
D. Correct
E. Period inside the quote: *"heart finger."*
F. Hyphen needed: The correct spelling is *left-hand*
G. Correct
H. Add comma after *murmur*
I. Correct
J. Comma after *poisonous*; an exclamation point after *iffy*—not a question mark
K. Correct
L. Period inside the quote: *"heart finger."*
M. Correct
N. No comma after *wore*
O. Correct

Chapter 2: Grammar—Clarity, Clarity, Clarity

A. adjective
B. verb
C. adverb
D. conjunction

E.   noun
F.   infinitive
G.   preposition

Chapter 3: Facts—The Acceptable and the Unacceptable

List of words and phrases plagiarized:

A.   satellite data sets; international team of university and NASA scientists
B.   surface temperature
C.   northern landscape
D.   3.5 million square miles (9 million sq km), which is an area about equal to the contiguous United States
E.   Throughout, the student author gives no attribution to where he found this information.

Chapter 4: Style—Create Unique Writing

A.   a form of the verb *to be* used in every sentence; no comma before *but*
B.   *it's* SHOULD be *its*
C.   subjunctive "if" phrase: If the sun *were*
D.   *rotate*—subject is plural
E.   capitalize *Equator*
F.   number style—use digits—*36*
G.   *increasingly* should be *increasing*
H.   the word *spacecraft* is one word
I.   incorrect fact—there are *eight* planets, not 12, that orbit the sun
J.   add "ly": *approximately*

Chapter 5: Voice—Every Writer's Goal

A.   classic—denotative, meaning excellent or the best of its kind
B.   challenges—denotative, meaning problems
        built—connotative—implies he shaped or formed his life
C.   new—connotative—implies he improved his life

D.   under her wing—connotative—implies that she looked out for him, helped him

      settling—connotative—implies deciding or reaching an agreement

E.   fell in love—connotative—he had deep loving feelings for Dora

      slight—denotative—thin, not strong

F.   childish—denotative—immature

      childlike—denotative—innocent

G.   snake—connotative—villain, evil

H.   now—denotative—meaning today

      vile—denotative—meaning evil

BIBLIOGRAPHY

Allen, Robert, ed. *Pocket Fowler's Modern English Usage*. New York: Oxford University Press, 2004.

American Experience. "Primary Resources: A Journalistic Masterpiece." PBS. Accessed September 9, 2013, http://www.pbs.org/wgbh/americanexperience/features/primary-resources/rockefellers-mcclures/.

American Library Association. "Using Primary Sources on the Web" and "Evaluating Primary Source Web Sites." Accessed November 18, 2013, http://www.ala.org/rusa/resources/usingprimarysources.

Aristotle. *The Poetics*. Translated by Stephen Halliwell. Cambridge, MA: Harvard University Press, 1995.

———. *Rhetoric and the Poetics*. Translated by W. Rhys Roberts and Ingram Bywater. New York: Random House, 1984.

———. *Rhetoric and the Poetics*. Cambridge, MA: MIT Classics. Accessed August 13, 2013, http://classics.mit.edu/Aristotle/rhetoric.3.iii.html.

Copland, Aaron. *What to Listen for in Music*. New York: A Mentor Book, Penguin, 1953.

Declaration of Independence. The U.S. National Archives & Record Administration. Accessed November 18, 2013, http://www.archives.gov/exhibits/charters/declaration_transcript.html.

Dickens, Charles. *A Tale of Two Cities*. Literature Project. Accessed August 15, 2013, http://www.literatureproject.com/tale-two-cities/tale2cities_1.htm.

Fennell, Francis L. *Collegiate English Handbook*. 5th ed. San Diego, CA: Collegiate Press, 2002.

Fowler, Ramsey H. *The Little, Brown Handbook*. 8th ed. New York: Longman, 2001.

BIBLIOGRAPHY

———. *The Little, Brown Handbook.* 9th ed. New York: Longman, 2004.

Garner, Bryan A. *The Oxford Dictionary of American Usage and Style.* New York: Oxford University Press, 2000.

Gibbon, Edward. *History of the Decline and Fall of the Roman Empire.* 6 vols. 1776–1788. Accessed September 12, 2013, http://www.Gutenberg.org/files/731/731-h/731-h.htm#link2HCH0001.

Hacker, Diana. *A Pocket Style Manual.* 5th ed. Boston: Bedford/St. Martin's, 2008.

Halliwell, Stephen. *Aristotle's Poetics.* Chicago: University of Chicago Press, 1986, 1998.

Jones, Peder, and Jay Farness. *College Writing Skills.* 4th ed. San Diego, CA: Collegiate Press, 1997.

Lanham, Richard A. *The Longman Guide to Revising Prose.* New York: Pearson, Longman, 2006.

McCrimmon, James M. *Writing with a Purpose.* 3rd ed. Boston: Houghton Mifflin, 1963.

Modern Language Association. *MLA Handbook for Writers of Research Papers.* 7th ed. New York: Modern Language Association of America, 2009.

———. *MLA Style Manual and Guide to Scholarly Publishing.* 3rd ed. New York: Modern Language Association of America, 2008.

Opdycke, John B. *Harper's English Grammar.* New York: Fawcett Popular Library, 1965.

Pratt, William. *The Imagist Poem: Modern Poetry in Miniature.* New York: Dutton, 1963.

Purdue Online Writing Lab (OWL). "Punctuation." Accessed August 10, 2013, http://owl.english.purdue.edu/owl/section/1/6/.

Smith, Sarah Harrison. *The Fact Checker's Bible.* New York: Random House, 2004.

Strumpf, Michael, and Auriel Douglas. *The Grammar Bible.* New York: Henry Holt, 2004.

Strunk, William, Jr., and E. B. White. *The Elements of Style.* New York: Longman, 2000.

Tarbell, Ida M. *The History of the Standard Oil Company.* Gloucester, MA: Peter Smith, 1963.

University of Chicago Press. *The Chicago Manual of Style.* 16th ed. Chicago: University of Chicago Press, 2010.

Williams, Joseph. *Style: Toward Clarity and Grace.* Chicago: University of Chicago Press, 1990.

Yagoda, Ben. *How to Not Write Bad.* New York: Penguin Group, 2013.

——. *The Sound on the Page*. Harper Resource. New York: HarperCollins, 2004.

Yale College Writing Center. "Common Knowledge." Accessed November 18, 2013, http://writing.yalecollege.yale.edu/common-knowledge.

——. "What Is Plagiarism?" Accessed November 18, 2013, http://writing.yale college.yale.edu/what-plagiarism.

Zinsser, William. *On Writing Well*. New York: Harper & Row, 1988.

INDEX

58, 60–61; reflexive, 59; relative, 58–59; usage essentials for, 57–61
proper nouns, 53
punctuation: American English nuances with, 39; clarity with, 4; concept of, 12–13; consistency with, 20; end or external, 13–16; essentials of, 13; first experiences learning, 11; with fragments, 16; importance of, 3–4; internal, 15, 17–38; mechanical style and, 107–8; signage and, 16–17; in Style Sheet, 135, 138; 21st-century changes in, 12; voice and, 118. *See also specific types*
punctuation, grammar, facts, style, voice system (PGFSV system), 3–6. *See also specific essentials*

qigong, 7
qualities, nouns and, 52–53
question marks: feeling conveyed by, 13–14; usage essentials for, 14–15
quotation marks, 34–35

reading, style improved by, 112
reference materials, Style Sheets, 134–35, 137–38
reflexive pronouns, 59
relative pronouns, 58–59
research: Elvis Presley example of, 80–81; of facts, 75–78; Google founding example of, 82–83; Hubble Space Telescope example for, 81–82; on Internet, 76–78; United States in Korean War example of, 79–80
restrictive commas, 25
Rhetoric (Aristotle), 100–101, 121

robocall, 8
Rockefeller, John D., 126, 127

secondary sources, 74; definition of, 76; in Elvis Presley research example, 81; Google founding research example, 83; in Hubble Space Telescope research example, 82; in United States in Korean War research example, 80; websites and, 76
semicolons, 12–13; essential usage of, 28–29; Internet and future of, 28
series commas, 19–20
signage, punctuation on, 16–17
Six Easy Commas, 18–28
slant and spin: of websites, 78; in writing style, 111–12
slashes, 37–38
sources: citing, 74, 83–84, 85, 108; keeping track of, 82; primary, 74, 75, 79–83; secondary, 74, 76, 80–83; websites as, 76–77
specificity, style and, 110–11
specific words, 120
spell-checking programs, passive voice and, 49
splice, comma, 21–22
Standard Oil Company, 126–30
statistics, 75
Strunk, William, Jr., 101
style: Aristotle's advice on, 101; clarity and, 100–102; content flow and, 113–14; definition of, 99; *Elements of Style* advice on, 101; essential points on, 100; mechanical, 6, 99, 102–8, 113; organization for, 112; reading improving, 112; recognition of, 99–100; slant and spin in, 111–12; specificity and,